OPPOSING
VIEWPOINTS®
SERIES

Mental Illness

Other Books of Related Interest:

Opposing Viewpoints Series

The Pharmaceutical Industry

At Issue Series

Are Americans Overmedicated?

Current Controversies Series

Alternative Therapies

"Congress shall make
no law . . . abridging
the freedom of speech,
or of the press."

First Amendment to the US Constitution

The basic foundation of our democracy is the First Amendment guarantee of freedom of expression. The *Opposing Viewpoints* series is dedicated to the concept of this basic freedom and the idea that it is more important to practice it than to enshrine it.

Mental Illness

Roman Espejo, Book Editor

GREENHAVEN PRESS
A part of Gale, Cengage Learning

GALE
CENGAGE Learning

Detroit • New York • San Francisco • New Haven, Conn • Waterville, Maine • London

GALE
CENGAGE Learning

Elizabeth Des Chenes, *Managing Editor*

© 2012 Greenhaven Press, a part of Gale, Cengage Learning.

Gale and Greenhaven Press are registered trademarks used herein under license.

For more information, contact:
Greenhaven Press
27500 Drake Rd.
Farmington Hills, MI 48331-3535
Or you can visit our Internet site at gale.cengage.com

For product information and technology assistance, contact us at

Gale Customer Support, 1-800-877-4253
For permission to use material from this text or product, submit all requests online at www.cengage.com/permissions

Further permissions questions can be emailed to permissionrequest@cengage.com

Articles in Greenhaven Press anthologies are often edited for length to meet page requirements. In addition, original titles of these works are changed to clearly present the main thesis and to explicitly indicate the author's opinion. Every effort is made to ensure that Greenhaven Press accurately reflects the original intent of the authors. Every effort has been made to trace the owners of copyrighted material.

Cover Image © Kentoh/Shutterstock.com.

LIBRARY OF CONGRESS CATALOGING-IN-PUBLICATION DATA

Mental illness / Roman Espejo, book editor.
    p. cm. -- (Opposing viewpoints)
    Summary: "Mental Illness: Is Mental Illness a Serious Problem?; How Should Society Address Mental Illness?; What Mental Health Issues Do Youths Face Today?; What Treatments for Mental Illness Are Effective?"-- Provided by publisher.
    Includes bibliographical references and index.
    ISBN 978-0-7377-5735-4 (hardback) -- ISBN 978-0-7377-5736-1 (paperback)
    1. Mental illness--Treatment. 2. Mental illness--Social aspects. I. Espejo, Roman, 1977-
    RC480.M46 2011
    362.2--dc22
                                            2011011655

Printed in the United States of America
1 2 3 4 5 6 7 15 14 13 12 11

Contents

Chapter 3: What Mental Health Issues Do Youths Face Today?

Chapter 4: What Treatments for Mental Illness Are Effective?

Why Consider Opposing Viewpoints?

> "The only way in which a human being can make some approach to knowing the whole of a subject is by hearing what can be said about it by persons of every variety of opinion and studying all modes in which it can be looked at by every character of mind. No wise man ever acquired his wisdom in any mode but this."
>
> John Stuart Mill

In our media-intensive culture it is not difficult to find differing opinions. Thousands of newspapers and magazines and dozens of radio and television talk shows resound with differing points of view. The difficulty lies in deciding which opinion to agree with and which "experts" seem the most credible. The more inundated we become with differing opinions and claims, the more essential it is to hone critical reading and thinking skills to evaluate these ideas. Opposing Viewpoints books address this problem directly by presenting stimulating debates that can be used to enhance and teach these skills. The varied opinions contained in each book examine many different aspects of a single issue. While examining these conveniently edited opposing views, readers can develop critical thinking skills such as the ability to compare and contrast authors' credibility, facts, argumentation styles, use of persuasive techniques, and other stylistic tools. In short, the Opposing Viewpoints Series is an ideal way to attain the higher-level thinking and reading skills so essential in a culture of diverse and contradictory opinions.

In addition to providing a tool for critical thinking, *Opposing Viewpoints* books challenge readers to question their own strongly held opinions and assumptions. Most people form their opinions on the basis of upbringing, peer pressure, and personal, cultural, or professional bias. By reading carefully balanced opposing views, readers must directly confront new ideas as well as the opinions of those with whom they disagree. This is not to simplistically argue that everyone who reads opposing views will—or should—change his or her opinion. Instead, the series enhances readers' understanding of their own views by encouraging confrontation with opposing ideas. Careful examination of others' views can lead to the readers' understanding of the logical inconsistencies in their own opinions, perspective on why they hold an opinion, and the consideration of the possibility that their opinion requires further evaluation.

Evaluating Other Opinions

To ensure that this type of examination occurs, *Opposing Viewpoints* books present all types of opinions. Prominent spokespeople on different sides of each issue as well as well-known professionals from many disciplines challenge the reader. An additional goal of the series is to provide a forum for other, less known, or even unpopular viewpoints. The opinion of an ordinary person who has had to make the decision to cut off life support from a terminally ill relative, for example, may be just as valuable and provide just as much insight as a medical ethicist's professional opinion. The editors have two additional purposes in including these less known views. One, the editors encourage readers to respect others' opinions—even when not enhanced by professional credibility. It is only by reading or listening to and objectively evaluating others' ideas that one can determine whether they are worthy of consideration. Two, the inclusion of such viewpoints encourages the important critical thinking skill of objectively evaluating an author's credentials and bias. This evaluation will illuminate an author's reasons for taking a particular stance on an issue and will aid in readers' evaluation of the author's ideas.

It is our hope that these books will give readers a deeper understanding of the issues debated and an appreciation of the complexity of even seemingly simple issues when good and honest people disagree. This awareness is particularly important in a democratic society such as ours in which people enter into public debate to determine the common good. Those with whom one disagrees should not be regarded as enemies but rather as people whose views deserve careful examination and may shed light on one's own.

Thomas Jefferson once said that "difference of opinion leads to inquiry, and inquiry to truth." Jefferson, a broadly educated man, argued that "if a nation expects to be ignorant and free . . . it expects what never was and never will be." As individuals and as a nation, it is imperative that we consider the opinions of others and examine them with skill and discernment. The *Opposing Viewpoints* series is intended to help readers achieve this goal.

David L. Bender and Bruno Leone,
Founders

Introduction

"Anxiety, which may be understood as the pathological counterpart of normal fear, is manifest by disturbances of mood, as well as of thinking, behavior, and physiological activity."

US Department of
Health and Human Services,
Mental Health: A Report of
the Surgeon General, 1999

"Anxiety [is] today wildly overdiagnosed and overtreated with usually inappropriate, often ineffective, and frequently dangerous products." .

*Vernon Coleman,
former general practitioner
and author of* How to Stop
Your Doctor Killing You

About forty million American adults have an anxiety disorder, or 18.1 percent of the general population eighteen and older, according to the National Institute of Mental Health (NIMH). "Anxiety is a normal reaction to stress. It helps one deal with a tense situation in the office, study harder for an exam, keep focused on an important speech," NIMH states on its website, adding that "when anxiety becomes an excessive, irrational dread of everyday situations, it has become a disabling disorder." There are five major types of anxiety disorders: generalized anxiety disorder (GAD), obsessive-compulsive disorder (OCD), panic disorder, post-traumatic stress disorder (PTSD), and social anxiety disorder.

GAD is marked by persistent anxiousness, a lack of focus, and magnified worries and concerns that persist for at least six months in the absence of reasonable sources of stress. Physical symptoms such as tiredness, headache, muscle pain, twitching, dizziness, and nausea may occur as well. People with GAD often live normal lives, but extreme instances of anxiety can hinder them from performing everyday tasks. "One fear begets another fear, begets another fear, and it continues in a vicious circle, wearing us down, making us feel unable to cope or exist in a 'normal' way," writes Amy Gates, a mother of two in recovery from GAD, in her blog *Crunchy Domestic Goddess*. An estimated 6.8 million Americans have been diagnosed with the disorder, which affects twice as many females as males.

Individuals with OCD have obsessive thoughts and engage in compulsive habits, or rituals, to deal with their obsessions. "Healthy people also have rituals, such as checking to see if the stove is off several times before leaving the house," maintains the NIMH website, which also explains "the difference is that people with OCD perform their rituals even though doing so interferes with daily life and they find the repetition distressing." For example social worker Bill Ford—profiled in an article by Mara Bovsun on BrainPhysics.com—stayed up an entire night in a hospital feeling ashtrays for burning cigarette butts in fears one would start a fire. "I had images of something terrible happening and of it being my fault," he says. "I was exhausted, paddling as hard as I could to keep my head above water." Approximately 2.2 million Americans live with OCD.

Panic disorder is distinguished by sudden attacks of overwhelming fear, with physical symptoms such as sweatiness, palpitations, and a sense of being suffocated. For some people the experience is so intense that they believe they are about to die or have a heart attack. "People who have full-blown, repeated panic attacks can become very disabled by their condition and should seek treatment before they start to avoid places or situations where panic attacks have occurred,"

NIMH's website states. For Amy Roberts, panic disorder dominated her everyday life for fifteen years. "There was always a fear in the back of my mind that, just maybe, this time it would be more than 'just' a panic attack," Roberts reveals on AnxietyPanic.com. Around six million people have been diagnosed with panic disorder.

PTSD follows a traumatic event or series of events in which a person is physically harmed or threatened with violence, such as sexual assault, warfare, and accidents. Individuals with PTSD become detached from family and friends, are easily frightened or provoked, and are often prone to aggression. They also become avoidant of environments that remind them of the event or have nightmares or flashbacks of the experience, which can be triggered by everyday sights and sounds. A survivor of childhood abuse, P.K. Philips experienced PTSD after an assault at knifepoint. "I saw violent images every time I closed my eyes. I lost all ability to concentrate or even complete simple tasks," she recalls in an article on the Anxiety Disorders Association of America (ADAA) website. The disorder impacts 7.7 million American adults.

People with social anxiety disorder, or social phobia, are excessively self-conscious and anxious in social situations. They constantly dread scrutiny, judgment, and embarrassment in public or in front of others. Physical symptoms include shaking, sweating, and difficulty in speaking. "Even if they manage to confront their fears and be around others," NIMH explains on its website, "they are usually very anxious beforehand, are intensely uncomfortable throughout the encounter, and worry about how they were judged for hours afterward." Despite playing football in packed stadiums, Ricky Williams, Miami Dolphins running back, feared encountering fans and shopping for groceries. "I was 23, a millionaire and had everything, yet I was never more unhappy in my life," he says in an article on the ADAA website. "I felt extremely isolated from my friends and family because I couldn't explain to them what I was feeling." More than fifteen million people have social phobia.

Experts cite a range of causes for anxiety disorders, including severe stress, chemical imbalances found in the body, and genetics. "Researchers are learning that anxiety disorders run in families, and that they have a biological basis, much like allergies or diabetes and other disorders," claims the ADAA's website. In opposition, critics dismiss the idea of anxiety as a widespread, or even real, illness. Simon Enoch, a doctoral student at Ryerson University, argues that diagnostic measures have changed, resulting in the growing prevalence of anxiety. "The case of social anxiety sufferers is just one small constituent part of the expanding horizon of psychiatric discourse," Enoch asserts in a 2005 article in *Theory and Science*, further adding, a part of "an increasing tendency within psychiatry to medicate away unwanted feelings or emotions."

In *Opposing Viewpoints: Mental Illness*, similar debates surrounding mental illness are investigated in the following chapters: Is Mental Illness a Serious Problem? How Should Society Address Mental Illness? What Mental Health Issues Do Youths Face Today? and What Treatments for Mental Illness Are Effective? The authors in this volume challenge and support how mental illness is defined and treated in the United States.

CHAPTER 1

Is Mental Illness a Serious Problem?

Chapter Preface

Major depression is prevalent in the United States, according to the National Institute of Mental Health (NIMH). The institute reports that it affects 14.8 million adults—6.7 percent of the population age eighteen and older each year—and is the most common cause of disability for persons between the ages of fifteen and forty-four. The onset of major depressive disorder starts at the median age of thirty-two, adds NIMH, and affects more women than men. "Major depression is disabling and prevents a person from functioning normally," explains the NIMH website. "An episode of major depression may occur only once in a person's lifetime, but more often, it recurs throughout a person's life."

Several forms of depression with distinct characteristics are recognized. Dysthymic disorder persists for two years or more, but is less debilitating than major depression. Minor depression is short-term and also less severe than major depression and dysthymic disorder. Psychotic depression accompanies forms of psychosis, in which a loss of touch with reality, hallucinations, or delusions are experienced. And seasonal affective disorder (SAD) is a type of depression that occurs during the winter, when exposure to sunlight is limited. "Depression often co-exists with other illnesses. Such illnesses may precede the depression, cause it, and/or be a consequence of it," claims the NIMH website.

Some experts argue that depression is overdiagnosed and normal feelings of sadness and negativity are being medicalized. "A low threshold for diagnosing clinical depression . . . risks normal human emotional states being treated as illness, challenging the model's credibility and risking inappropriate management," contends Australian psychiatrist Gordon Parker in his August 18, 2007, article in the *British Medical Journal*. "Depression is a diagnosis that will remain a non-specific 'catch all' until common sense brings current confusion to order." In the following viewpoints, the authors discuss the scope of mental illness across the nation and as a social problem.

"I challenge you to find any family, during a family's lifetime, that doesn't have some kind of mental health problem."

Mental Illness Is Prevalent in America

Marla Cantrell

Marla Cantrell is a writer for the City Wire *in Fort Smith, Arkansas. In the following viewpoint, Cantrell purports that one in five Americans will suffer from a mental illness in his or her lifetime, with up to 9 percent of the population developing a serious disorder. But facing psychiatric stigma, many states lack evidence-based treatment, mental health courts, and law enforcement trained to deal with the mentally ill, Cantrell claims. As a result, the costs of treating mental illnesses, she continues, are a burden to families and state government.*

As you read, consider the following questions:

1. What average grade did the National Alliance on Mental Illness (NAMI) give to the nation's mental health care systems?

2. How did Jack Baker and Lisa Huckelbury afford treatment for their schizophrenic son?

3. How much does NAMI estimate that untreated mental illness costs America per year?

Mental illness is something we whisper about, hoping the neighbors don't hear. We skirt around the issue at family gatherings when we're asked why Jennie is still living at home, why Sam refuses to leave his room, why Joe keeps ending up on the news.

But it's out there on every corner, and if it hasn't yet visited your family, it probably will.

The National Alliance on Mental Illness (NAMI) reports that one in five people will be diagnosed with a mental disorder at some time in his or her life, and that 5% to 9% of the population will develop a serious mental condition.

Arkansas Rep. Tracy Pennartz, D-Fort Smith, spent more than two decades in behavioral health care. She understands the problem.

"I challenge you to find any family, during a family's lifetime, that doesn't have some kind of mental health problem," Pennartz said. "Not a mental illness maybe but a mental health problem. For example, here in Fort Smith, we had a lot of people laid off from work. To expect them not to be depressed about that is unrealistic. And in some cases, if the depression is prolonged, they may seek out mental health counseling for that."

Failing Grade

The issue crosses every socioeconomic boundary. But its prevalence is not enough to crush the stigma attached to it, or keep Arkansas from getting a failing grade in corralling it. In March [2009], NAMI gave the state an F, citing problems such as lack of implementing evidence-based practices to treat mental illness, no mental health courts—which would work in much the same way as drug courts—and a deficiency in law enforcement training. In 2006, Arkansas was given a D- from NAMI. Arkansas was one of six states receiving a failing grade. Oklahoma received a B. No state received and A and the national average was a D.

Kim Arnold, executive director of NAMI Arkansas, said they appreciate the challenges officers face in dealing with the mentally ill.

"We're not saying the police aren't doing what they're trained to do, but we are saying the police are losing one valuable piece in this," Arnold said. "How do you recognize mental illness? How do you treat a person who has a mental illness? Crisis Intervention Team, which was developed in Memphis, pairs up mental health professionals and police officers to actually do this together. It's about a 40-hour course that trains a police officer how to recognize symptoms or situations where a person could be experiencing a mental illness or episode where the person is behaving in an erratic or very disorganized way."

In 2007, the Arkansas legislature passed an act that required the Criminal Justice Institute to write a curriculum and help train officers. NAMI didn't understand why another program was being developed when the Crisis Intervention Team program already existed. And that bill did not make the training mandatory.

The Fort Smith Police Department does receive training both at the academy and in follow-up refresher courses.

"We've sent a division commander to training and he teaches a refresher course on it every three years," Fort Smith Police Sergeant Jim Harris said. "There's no set standard on how much training we get, so it's up to the academy on how much they present. . . . We could always use more training in everything. We just don't have enough time in the day. The fact that we do it every three years is more than some agencies get to do."

Lt. Brent Grill, with the Van Buren Police Department, said his department struggles because the city doesn't have a facility for those with mental illnesses.

"The problem we, as law enforcement, deal with is there is no place in Van Buren to take someone that may need help with their mental illness," Grill said. "If the person is a threat to him- or herself at the time that makes things a little different. The average person who is mentally ill probably will not get assistance from law enforcement. . . . I will say that this subject is often discussed and what law enforcement needs to do. Recognizing the problem and what area law enforcement has the authority to do, is the question that has not been answered."

A report by the Bazelon Center [for Mental Health Law] released in June [2009] found 14.5% of men and 31% of women in the jails they studied had serious mental illnesses. It's a large number. In 2007, 13 million Americans spent time in jail.

Family Costs

Jack Baker, facilitator for the Fort Smith NAMI support group, has met a police officer or two since his son was diagnosed with schizophrenia. Fourteen years ago he and his wife Lisa Huckelbury realized one of their five sons was mentally ill. There were episodes of violence. And he was a strong boy— 6'4" and 240 pounds. The couple didn't know what to do. They searched for help, but found little. The teen was eventually diagnosed with schizophrenia. Today, he lives in a facility in Hot Springs and is doing well.

While dealing with the chaos, the family also had to worry about their bank account.

"We saw real quick we were going to have to take advantage of state funding through Social Security Disability," Baker said. "He had numerous files and so it was a fight getting him on there. That allows you to take them to different facilities and have them in-house treated. It's about the only way to afford mental illness. Otherwise, you're spending ten grand ($10,000) a month."

Arnold said the burden for families like Baker's are great.

"There are many in our state that will accept pay sources such as insurance, Medicaid or Medicare but very few that will accept persons with no insurance and then offer a fee reduction or a sliding fee scale," Arnold said. "Those places that are federally mandated to do so are the Community Mental Health Centers in our state and they are throughout the state in 15 catchment areas."

State Costs

The state tries, Arnold said, but falling revenues continue to be a problem.

"Community Mental Health Centers are mandated to see and treat persons who have no pay source, but they have not had many, if any, increases in what they receive in funding to do that for quite some time," Arnold said. "Yet they have endured cuts in funds and increases in those who fall into that category."

Pennartz believes Arkansas is doing a good job addressing the issue and Fort Smith is doing particularly well.

"We are fortunate in Fort Smith. We're the state's second largest city and a health care provider not just for the city but for the region," Pennartz said. "We provide services for people within 60 minutes from the city. We have two major medical centers. . . . And there are in excess of 60 mental health care clinics across the state."

The Arkansas Division of Behavioral Health Services, which includes the Arkansas Health Center, reports its total biennial budget for 2009–11 as $165.34 million the first year and $166.02 million the second. The division also runs the Alcohol and Drug Abuse Prevention Program.

Suicide Reporting

NAMI said mental disorders are the leading cause of disability and without treatment the effects are staggering. NAMI estimates the cost of untreated mental illness is $100 billion dollars per year in the U.S. Further, those affected can face homelessness, incarceration, substance abuse and suicide.

Baker cringes at the thought of those lost lives. Just two weeks ago [in late 2009] he lost his first group member to suicide.

"I lost my first one two weeks ago after twelve years," Baker said, wiping away tears. "I helped her every day. She was like a kid. A 46-year-old kid."

The Van Buren man has a radical idea for local newspapers. He wants them to report suicides so that the breadth of the problem can be brought to light.

Baker and Arnold are watching the health care reform bill closely. Arnold said NAMI supported the House bill and is waiting to see what changes evolve in the Senate's version.

In the meantime, Baker is offering help of his own. It's called the Family to Family program he now helps teach during NAMI support meetings in Fort Smith.

"It changed our life," Baker said. "It educated us about mental illness, not only the different types but the characteristics of each disorder. If we hadn't gone to that we probably would have lost it. It was a very frustrating five-year period there. We got through it, but it was a living hell."

"In this brave new world of psychiatric overdiagnosis, will anyone get through life without a mental disorder?"

The Prevalence of Mental Illness in America Is Exaggerated

Allen Frances

Allen Frances was chair of the Diagnostic and Statistical Manual of Mental Disorders, Fourth Edition *(DSM-IV) Task Force and the psychiatry department at Duke University School of Medicine. In the following viewpoint, Frances contends that Americans are overdiagnosed with mental disorders as a result of current diagnostic measures. According to him, the criteria for mental disorders are too inclusive and easier to meet, advocacy groups inadvertently lead to the mislabeling of mental disorders, and psychiatry websites compel individuals to diagnose themselves.*

As you read, consider the following questions:

1. How does Frances respond to the assertion that the stresses of modern life increase the likelihood of mental disorders?

2. What role does the pharmaceutical industry play in epidemics of mental illnesses, in the author's opinion?

3. How does society encourage psychiatric overdiagnosis, in the author's view?

Fads in psychiatric diagnosis come and go and have been with us as long as there has been psychiatry. The fads meet a deeply felt need to explain, or at least to label, what would otherwise be unexplainable human suffering and deviance. In recent years the pace has picked up and false "epidemics" have come in bunches involving an ever-increasing proportion of the population. We are now in the midst of at least 3 such epidemics—of autism, attention deficit, and childhood bipolar disorder. And unless it comes to its senses, DSM-5 threatens to provoke several more (hypersexuality, binge eating, mixed anxiety depression, minor neurocognitive, and others).

Fads punctuate what has become a basic background of overdiagnosis. Normality is an endangered species. The NIMH estimates that, in any given year, 25 percent of the population (that's almost 60 million people) has a diagnosable mental disorder. A prospective study found that, by age thirty-two, 50 percent of the general population had qualified for an anxiety disorder, 40 percent for depression, and 30 percent for alcohol abuse or dependence. Imagine what the rates will be like by the time these people hit fifty, or sixty-five, or eighty. In this brave new world of psychiatric overdiagnosis, will anyone get through life without a mental disorder?

What accounts for the recent upsurge in diagnosis? I feel quite confident we can't blame it on our brains. Human physiology and human nature change slowly if at all. Could it be that the surge in mental disorders is caused by our stressful society? I think not. There is no particular reason to believe that life is any harder now than it has always been—more likely we are the most pampered and protected generation ever to face its inevitable challenges. It is also tempting to find environmental (e.g., toxins) or iatrogenic causes (e.g., vaccinations), but there is no credible evidence supporting either of these. There is really only one viable environmental candidate to explain the growth of mental disorder—the widespread recreational use of psychotropic substances. But this cannot account for the extent of the "epidemics," particularly since most have centered on children.

No. The "epidemics" in psychiatry are caused by changing diagnostic fashions—the people don't change, the labels do. There are no objective tests in psychiatry—no X-ray, laboratory, or exam that says definitively that someone does or does not have a mental disorder. What is diagnosed as mental disorder is very sensitive to professional and social contextual forces. Rates of disorder rise easily because mental disorder has such fluid boundaries with normality.

What are the most important contextual forces?

1. DSM-III made psychiatric diagnosis interesting and accessible to the general public. More than a million copies of each edition have been sold—more to ordinary people than to mental health professionals. The widespread appeal of the DSM is in its clear definitions that allow people to diagnose themselves and family members. For the most part, this has been a useful contributor to self-knowledge and to early identification and treatment. But it can also be overdone and inevitably leads to overdiagnosis in the hands of non-clinicians.

2. This interacts with the fact that it is fairly easy to meet criteria for one or another DSM diagnosis. The definitional thresholds may be set too low and the DSM system has included many new diagnoses that are very common in the general population. The experts who establish the DSM criteria

Medicalizing Human Experience

All cultures struggle with intractable mental illnesses with varying degrees of compassion and cruelty, equanimity and fear. Looking at ourselves through the eyes of those living in places where madness and psychological trauma are still embedded in complex religious and cultural narratives, however, we get a glimpse of ourselves as an increasingly insecure and fearful people. Some philosophers and psychiatrists have suggested that we are investing our great wealth in researching and treating mental illness—medicalizing ever larger swaths of human experience—because we have rather suddenly lost older belief systems that once gave meaning and context to mental suffering.

If our rising need for mental health services does indeed spring from a breakdown of meaning, our insistence that the rest of the world think like us may be all the more problematic. Offering the latest Western mental health theories, treatments and categories in an attempt to ameliorate the psychological stress sparked by modernization and globalization is not a solution; it may be part of the problem. When we undermine local conceptions of the self and modes of healing, we may be speeding along the disorienting changes that are at the very heart of much of the world's mental distress.

Ethan Watters,
"The Americanization of Mental Illness,"
New York Times, *January 8, 2010.*

always worry more about missing cases than about casting too wide a net and capturing people who do not require a diagnosis or a treatment.

3. The pharmaceutical industry has proven to be fairly unsuccessful in developing new and improved medications. But it is wonderfully effective at marketing existing wares and is an important engine in overdiagnosis and the spread of psychiatric epidemics. The drug companies are skilled at mounting a full-court press that includes "educating" doctors, "supporting" advocacy groups and professional associations, controlling research, and direct-to-consumer advertising.

4. Patient and family advocacy groups have played an important role in calling attention to neglected needs; in lobbying for clinical, school, and research programs; and in reducing stigma and promoting group and community support. There are times, however, when advocating for those with a disorder can spill over and promote the spread of the disorder to others who are mislabeled. The mental disorders all have unclear boundaries among themselves and with normality. Clinical experience and caution are necessary in distinguishing at the boundary who does and who does not meet the criteria for the diagnosis. Well-informed self-diagnosis or family diagnosis can play a screening role and is part of being a wise consumer. But self-diagnosis is usually far too inclusive and needs trimming and validation by a cautious clinician.

5. It is no accident that the recent "epidemics" have all occurred in the childhood disorders. There are two contributing factors. The first is the push by drug companies into this new market. The second is that the provision of special educational services often requires that there be a DSM diagnosis.

6. The Internet is a wonderful communication tool that provides a wealth of information and creates a social network of informed consumers. But it can also contribute to the spread of "epidemics." Disorder-focused websites (often run by patients and families) provide a powerfully attractive forum and support system that draws people who may inaccurately self-overdiagnose in order to be part of the Internet community.

7. The media feeds off and feeds the public interest in mental disorders. This happens in two ways. Periodically, the media becomes obsessed with one or another celebrity whose public meltdown seems related to a real or imagined mental disorder. The mental disorder is then endlessly commented on and dissected by the media. The latest example is the Tiger Woods media frenzy which will likely lead to an "epidemic" of "sexual addiction." Popular movies can also be contagious. *Sybil* helped cause a fad in multiple-personality disorder.

8. We live in a society that is perfectionistic in its expectations and intolerant of what were previously considered to be normal and expectable distress and individual difference. What was once accepted as the aches and pains of everyday life is now frequently labeled a mental disorder and treated with a pill. Eccentrics who would have been accepted on their own terms are now labeled as sick (with Asperger's) and in need of therapeutic intervention. Mental disorder labels can provide cover for societal problems. Criminal behavior has been medicalized (e.g., rape as a psychiatric disorder) because prison sentences are too short and such labeling allows for indefinite psychiatric commitment.

All the above factors interact to produce follow-the-leader diagnostic fads that punctuate a general pattern of overdiagnosis. The definition of fad is "a temporary fashion, notion, manner of conduct especially one followed enthusiastically by a group." What makes something a psychiatric fad is that a psychiatric label seems to explain some common, nonspecific, problematic symptom or behavior, and that label is suddenly given to everyone. The fact that everyone is doing it reduces the stigma of the diagnosis and leads to more people getting the diagnosis. Then, like the old adage that if you have a hammer, everything looks like a nail, the new label gets twisted to fit cases which really don't fit it simply because the label itself is popular and accepted.

There is no objective way to determine what should be the proper rate of mental disorder in the general population. My view is that DSM-IV is almost certainly overinclusive, but I would not recommend tightening the criteria until we have clear evidence this would do more good than harm. The DSM-5 bias to thrust open the diagnostic floodgates is supported only by flimsy evidence that does not come close to warranting its great risks of harmful unintended consequences. It is too bad that there is no advocacy group for normality that could effectively push back against all the forces aligned to expand the reach of mental disorders.

> *"If 'wonder drugs' like Prozac are really helping people, why has the number of Americans on government disability due to mental illness skyrocketed from 1.25 million in 1987 to over 4 million today?"*

Medications for Mental Illness Are Overprescribed

Robert Whitaker, as told to Jed Lipinski

Robert Whitaker is a journalist and author of Anatomy of an Epidemic: Magic Bullets, Psychiatric Drugs, and the Astonishing Rise of Mental Illness in America. *Jed Lipinski is a writer based in Brooklyn, New York. In the following viewpoint, Whitaker argues that psychiatric drugs are overprescribed in America, harming the patients who do not need them. He asserts that researchers have long established that medications for schizophrenia, anxiety, and attention deficit hyperactive disorder have poor recovery rates and are linked to complications and worsening symptoms. Nonetheless, Whitaker maintains, leading profession-*

Jed Lipinski, "Anatomy of an Epidemic: The Hidden Damage of Psychiatric Drugs," Salon.com, April 7, 2010. This article first appeared in Salon.com, at http://www.salon.com. An online version remains in the *Salon* archives. Reprinted with permission.

als and organizations refuse to change the image of psychiatric drugs as safe and effective and mental illnesses as biological ailments.

As you read, consider the following questions:

1. According to Whitaker, how does mental health treatment in the United States compare to developing countries?

2. What are the possible adverse effects of Ritalin, as described by Whitaker?

3. What are Whitaker's recommendations for using psychiatric drugs?

In the past few months, the perennial controversy over psychiatric drug use has been growing considerably more heated. A January study showed a negligible difference between antidepressants and placebos in treating all but the severest cases of depression. The study became the subject of a *Newsweek* cover story, and the value of psychiatric drugs has recently been debated in the pages of the *New Yorker*, the *New York Times* and *Salon*. Many doctors and patients fiercely defend psychiatric drugs and their ability to improve lives. But others claim their popularity is a warning sign of a dangerously overmedicated culture.

The timing of Robert Whitaker's *Anatomy of an Epidemic*, a comprehensive and highly readable history of psychiatry in the United States, couldn't be better. An acclaimed mental health journalist and winner of a George Polk Award for his reporting on the psychiatric field, Whitaker draws on 50 years of literature and in-person interviews with patients to answer a simple question: If "wonder drugs" like Prozac are really helping people, why has the number of Americans on government disability due to mental illness skyrocketed from 1.25 million in 1987 to over 4 million today?

Anatomy of an Epidemic is the first book to investigate the long-term outcomes of patients treated with psychiatric drugs, and Whitaker finds that, overall, the drugs may be doing more harm than good. Adhering to studies published in prominent medical journals, he argues that, over time, patients with schizophrenia do better off medication than on it. Children who take stimulants for ADHD, he writes, are more likely to suffer from mania and bipolar disorder than those who go unmedicated. Intended to challenge the conventional wisdom about psychiatric drugs, *Anatomy* is sure to provoke a hot-tempered response, especially from those inside the psychiatric community.

Salon spoke with Robert Whitaker over the phone about the reasons behind the pharmaceutical revolution, how "anxiety" became rebranded as "depression," and what he thinks psychiatrists are hiding from the American public.

Psychiatric drug use is a notoriously tough subject for writers, because of all the contradictory research. Why wade into it?

In 1998, I was writing a series for the *Boston Globe* on abuse of psychiatric patients in research settings. I came across the World Health Organization's outcomes study for schizophrenia patients, and found that outcomes were better for poor countries of the world—like India, Colombia, Nigeria—than for the rich countries. And I was startled to find that only a small percentage of patients in those countries were medicated. I also discovered that the number of people on disability for mental illness in this country has tripled over the last 20 years.

If our psychiatric drugs are effective at preventing mental illness, I thought, why are we getting so many people unable to work? I felt we needed to look at long-term outcomes and ask: What does the evidence show? Are we improving long-term outcomes or not?

But you claim in the book that psychiatrists have long known that these drugs can cause harm.

In the late 1970s, Jonathan Cole—the father of American psychopharmacology—wrote a paper called "Is the Cure Worse than the Disease?" that signaled that antipsychotics weren't the lifesaving drugs that people had hoped. In it, he reviewed all of the long-term harm the drugs could cause and observed that studies had shown that at least 50 percent of all schizophrenia patients could fare well without the drugs. He wrote, "Every schizophrenic outpatient maintained on antipsychotic medication should have the benefit of an adequate trial without drugs." This would save many from the dangers of tardive dyskinesia—involuntary body movements—as well as the financial and social burdens of prolonged drug therapy. The title of the paper poignantly sums up the awful long-term paradox.

Why didn't this change people's minds about psychiatric drugs?

Psychiatry essentially shut off any further public discussion of this sort. And there's a reason for this. In the 1970s, psychiatry felt that it was in a fight for its survival. Its two prominent classes of drugs—antipsychotics, and benzodiazepines like Valium—were coming to be seen as problematic and even harmful, and sales of these drugs declined. At the same time, there'd been an explosion in the number of counselors and psychologists offering other forms of nondrug therapy.

Psychiatry saw itself in competition for patients with these other therapists, and in the late 1970s, the field realized that its advantage in the marketplace was its prescribing powers. Thus the field consciously sought to tell a public story that would support the use of its medications, and embraced the "medical model" of psychiatric disorders. This took off with the publication of the *Diagnostic and Statistical Manual of Mental Disorders III* in 1980, which introduced many new classes of "treatable" disorders.

In a recent New Yorker article, Louis Menand suggested that anxiety drugs were rebranded as antidepressants in the '80s, because anxiety drugs had acquired a bad name. Is that really true?

Depression and anxiety are pretty closely linked. Before benzodiazepines came out, the discomfort that younger people and working people felt was seen as anxiety, by and large. Depression was seen as less common, a disease among the middle-aged and older. It was this deep thing, where people are putting their heads in their hands and can't move. But when the benzodiazepines were proven to be addictive and harmful, the pharmaceutical companies said, in essence, "We have this market of people who feel discomfort in their lives, which we used to call anxiety. If we can rebrand it as depression, then we can bring a new antidepressant to market." It was a reconceptualization of discomfort, and it opened up the giant market for antidepressants as we see today.

And yet many studies have shown that antidepressants can treat depression, especially in severe cases.

In severe cases, you do see that people benefit from antidepressants, and that shows up consistently. But you still have to raise the question, even in that severe group: What happens to those medicated patients in the long term, compared to what happened in previous times? One thing that surprised me, looking at the epidemiological literature from the pre-antidepressant era, is that even severely depressed, hospitalized patients could with time expect to get well, and most did. Today, however, there's a high incidence of patients on long-term drug therapy that become chronically ill.

What about stimulants used to treat ADHD. How effective are they?

These stimulants alter behavior in a way that teachers can appreciate. They subdue finger-tapping and disruptive symptoms. But in the 1990s, the National Institute of Mental Health started looking to see if things like Ritalin were benefiting kids with ADHD, and to this day they have no evidence that this drug treatment improves long-term functioning in any domain—the ADHD symptoms, lower delinquency rates, better performance at school, et cetera. Then the NIMH studied whether these drugs provide a long-term benefit, and they found that after three years, being on medication is actually a marker of deterioration. Some patients' growth has been stunted, their ADHD symptoms have worsened. William Pelham, from the State University of New York at Buffalo and one of the principal investigators in that study, said, "We need to confess to parents that we've found no benefit." None. And we think that with drugs, the benefits should outweigh the risks.

What's so risky about Ritalin?

For one, a significant percentage—between 10 and 25 percent—of kids prescribed medication for ADHD will have a manic episode or psychotic episode and deteriorate in such a way that they're diagnosed with bipolar disorder. A similar study in 2000 on pediatric bipolar disorder reported that 84 percent of the children treated for bipolar illness—at the Luci Bini Mood Disorders Clinic in New York—had been previously exposed to psychiatric medications. The author, Gianni Faedda, wrote, "Strikingly, in fewer than 10 percent of the cases was diagnosis of bipolar disorder considered initially." The reality is that until children were medicated with stimulants and antidepressants, you didn't see juvenile bipolar mania.

But if these studies are so groundbreaking, why have they gone unreported in the media?

Because the NIMH didn't announce it. Just as they didn't announce the 2007 outcome study for schizophrenia patients. In that study, the recovery rate was 40 percent for those off meds, but only 5 percent for those on meds. I checked all the NIMH press releases for 2007 and found no release on this study. I found no announcement of it in any American Psychiatric Association publication or textbook. Not a single newspaper published an account of the study. And that's because the psychiatric establishment—the NIMH, the APA, even the National Alliance on Mental Illness, an advocacy organization—did not put out any press release about it or try to alert the media in any way.

Are you suggesting that psychiatrists are beholden to pharmaceutical companies?

Not exactly, although most of the leading academic psychiatrists act as consultants, advisors and speakers for them. The problem is that psychiatry, starting in 1980 with the publication of the DSM-III, decided to tell the public that psychiatric disorders were biological ailments, and that its drugs were safe and effective treatments for those ailments. If it suddenly announces to the public that a long-term NIMH-funded study found that the 15-year recovery rate for schizophrenia patients was 40 percent for those off meds and 5 percent for those on meds, then that story begins to fall apart. By not reporting the results, psychiatry maintains the image of its drugs in the public mind, and the value of psychiatrists in today's therapy marketplace.

So do you think psychiatric drugs should be used at all?

I think they should be used in a selective, cautious manner. It should be understood that they're not fixing any chemical imbalances. And honestly, they should be used on a short-term basis. But beyond this, I think we should look at programs that are getting very good results. This is what I love about Keropudas Hospital's program in Finland. They have 20 years of great results treating newly psychotic patients. They see if patients can get better without the use of meds, and if they can't, then they try them. It's a best-use model, not a no-use or anti-med model. It fits with our studies done in the 1970s that found if you use this model, you get better outcomes, and a good number of people get better and go on with their lives.

"For many mental health consumers, access to the full range of the most effective medications is a crucial component of successful treatment and recovery."

Restricting Medications for Mental Illness Harms Patients

Mental Health America

In the following viewpoint, Mental Health America (MHA) promotes patients' access to psychiatric drugs that are medically necessary. MHA suggests that policies such as preferred drug lists based on costs, "fail-first" requirements that prevent coverage of other treatment options, and monthly prescription limits hinder recovery from mental disorders. The association recommends prescription practices based on clinical evidence, treatment protocols for medication prescribing, and exempting psychiatric drugs from preferred drug lists. Formerly known as the National Mental Health Association, MHA is a nonprofit advocacy group based in Alexandria, Virginia.

As you read, consider the following questions:

1. As stated by MHA, what do restrictive medication policies fail to acknowledge about consumers and physicians?

Mental Health America, "Position Statement 32: Access to Medications," September 18, 2010. Copyright © 2010 Mental Health America. Reproduced by permission.

2. What are algorithms in the context of medication prescribing, as described by MHA?

3. In MHA's view, how should preferred drug lists be developed and revised?

Mental Health America (MHA) envisions a society in which all people in need have access to the full array of high quality, community-based, culturally and linguistically competent, integrated mental health and substance abuse services, regardless of ability to pay. For many mental health consumers, access to the full range of the most effective medications is a crucial component of successful treatment and recovery. Such medically necessary psychotropic medications, and their combination with other services and supports, are often essential to permit people with mental health and substance use conditions to recover and to lead healthy and productive lives in their communities.

MHA opposes policies that restrict access to medically necessary medications. Such policies, which include preferred drug lists with prior authorization requirements, restrictive formularies, fail-first requirements, monthly prescription limits, and tiered co-payment structures, not only fail to achieve their intended purpose of reducing overall health care costs but prolong human suffering, and reduce the potential for an individual with a mental health or substance use condition to achieve full recovery. Moreover, restrictive policies fail to acknowledge that physicians and consumers should make individualized treatment decisions, recognizing the unique and non-interchangeable nature of human beings and psychotropic medications, and acknowledging that lack of access to medications has both human and fiscal consequences.

Background

MHA recognizes that health care administrators are faced with the challenge of containing costs while maintaining or improving the quality of the care provided to consumers. MHA supports state efforts to implement utilization management strategies that promote and improve the quality of care for individuals with mental health and substance use conditions while seeking containment and reduction of pharmaceutical costs to state Medicaid and other public health programs. Such strategies—which are premised on open access to all medications approved for the treatment of mental health conditions—include closer scrutiny of utilization data to manage cases of polypharmacy, fraud and abuse; provider education initiatives targeted at high volume prescribers; disease management programs; best practice prescribing edits; and algorithms and other practice standards that promote appropriate prescribing based on clinical data and evidence-based practice. Additionally, MHA supports the use of tools to enhance appropriate prescribing and other treatment practices in light of best practice models. Sophisticated modeling and the appropriate use of consumer and professional boards can assure credibility in the prescription of medicine as well as assuring consideration of the full range of treatment options and the active involvement of consumers in treatment decisions.

MHA believes that decisions should always be clinically based and that best practice prescribing will provide long-term cost containment. If implemented based upon the evidence, the practices and tools identified above can be useful for policy makers, practitioners, and consumers to ensure appropriate access to and prescribing of medications leading to quality improvement and cost containment.

- *Best practice prescribing edits* are intended to promote adherence to accepted mental health medication regimens as well as ensure safe and effective use. Edits are not formulary restrictions, but rather utilize clinical evidence to encourage quality and effective prescribing by preventing therapeutic duplication, overdosing, sub-

therapeutic dosing, and adverse medication-related reactions. Claims data can be reviewed to identify any
providers who appear to have unsafe or inappropriate
prescribing practices. This practice of processing edits
should identify problems or inconsistencies with the
clinical evidence around drug interactions, frequency of
refills, dose optimization, day's supply, and quantities
dispensed. Once identified, those providers with prescribing practices that are not clinically based can be
targeted for training on best practices and monitored
for fraud and abuse.

- *Algorithms* are treatment protocols for medication prescribing, guiding a practitioner with regard to what
drug to try first, and in turn, if it is not effective, which
medications can subsequently be prescribed. Algorithms
that are clinically based are especially helpful for those
providers with less expertise with treating mental illnesses, like primary care providers. If used appropri-
ately, algorithms may help in providing a more thorough and informed clinical response, potentially leading
to greater long-term use of outpatient services instead
of hospital and institutional care. Algorithms can also
define where a new medication fits in the sequence of
steps for optimal clinical outcomes. It is important to
remember that while algorithms can help assist the clinician in clinical decision making, they must be voluntary, and they are not a substitute for clinical judgment
and common sense. A well-constructed medication algorithm is not a cookbook for care, but can guide the
clinician through multiple treatment options. By including prior history, consumer preference, and past
responses in each step of the algorithm, a clinician can
tailor the treatment to an individual consumer's needs
with the goal of achieving full remission, community
integration, and recovery. Like other clinical tools, algo-

rithms should not be based on a fail-first mentality, use cost rather than clinical evidence as a determiner, or specify which brand of drug is preferable.

- *Consumer and professional boards* are yet another venue for monitoring the appropriate prescribing of mental health medications. A consumer and professional board can be established by statute to review and implement the coverage practices of state Medicaid plans and the prescribing practices of providers to ensure safety and improve adherence, quality and outcomes. The board may make recommendations based on peer-reviewed medical literature, observational studies, health economic studies, and input from physicians and patients. An effective board also recommends prescribing edits that are consistent with best practice and clinical evidence.

Consumer Protection

Recognizing that many states have already implemented a preferred drug list, MHA supports the exemption of all medications used to treat mental health and substance use conditions from prior authorization requirements. Such an exemption should address all classes and not include limits based on diagnosis. Moreover, states that have implemented preferred drug lists and other restrictive policies should ensure that the following consumer protection policies exist and are enforced:

- No "fail-first" requirements;

- Prescribers should have the option to designate "Dispense As Written" to prevent automatic switching at the pharmacy point-of-sale;

- A "grandfathering" policy should exist to ensure that consumers who are successfully being treated on a non-preferred medication are not forced to switch.

- Preferred drug lists should be developed and revised based on clinical evidence and scientific consensus taking into account efficacy, safety, and cost;

- Utilization management strategies should be developed by a Pharmacy & Therapeutics Committee that includes practicing physicians in the field of mental health and substance abuse treatment;

- The process for developing state utilization management strategies should include meaningful involvement from consumers and adequate opportunity for public input;

- Prior authorization should be timely and efficient so as not to delay access to medication, nor to deter the prescriber from ordering medications that will have optimal benefits;

- Appeals and grievance procedures must be clearly disseminated to beneficiaries subject to restrictions and must be both accessible and timely.

> "Creative minds in all kinds of areas, from science to poetry, and mathematics to humour, may have traits associated with psychosis."

Mental Illness Can Be a Source of Creativity

Roger Dobson

Roger Dobson is a journalist based in the United Kingdom. In the following viewpoint, Dobson argues that links between mental illness and creativity exist; prominent poets suffer more from mood disorders, and psychiatric patients excel in abstract thinking. Dobson proposes that the unusual and unconventional thought processes of psychosis could fuel problem solving and creative genius. In fact, he claims that mathematicians have an autistic-like preoccupation with detail, and comedians rely on humor as a coping mechanism against depression.

As you read, consider the following questions:

1. As stated in the viewpoint, how did mental disorders survive through evolution?

2. According to Dobson, how much more likely were major British and Irish poets to have suffered from mood disorders, suicide, and institutionalization during the seventeenth and eighteenth centuries?

3. How does Dobson characterize Salvador Dali?

At first glance, [Albert] Einstein, Salvador Dali, Tony Hancock, and Beach Boy Brian Wilson would seem to have little in common. Their areas of physics, modern art, comedy, and rock music are light-years apart. So what, if anything, could possibly link minds that gave the world the theory of relativity, great surreal art, iconic comedy, and songs about surfing?

According to new research, psychosis could be the answer. Creative minds in all kinds of areas, from science to poetry, and mathematics to humour, may have traits associated with psychosis. Such traits may allow the unusual and sometimes bizarre thought processes associated with mental illness to fuel creativity. The theory is based on the idea that there is no clear dividing line between the healthy and the mentally ill. Rather, there is a continuum, with some people having psychotic traits without having the debilitating symptoms.

Mental illnesses have been around for thousands of years. Evolutionary theory suggests that in order for them to be still here, there must be some kind of survival advantage to them. If they were wholly bad, it's argued, natural selection would have seen them off long ago. In some cases the advantage is clear. Anxiety, for example, can be a mental illness with severe symptoms and consequences, but it is also a trait that at a non-clinical level has survival advantages. In healthy proportions, it keeps us alert and on our toes when threats are sensed.

It's now increasingly being argued that there are survival advantages to others forms of illness, too, because of the links between the traits associated with them and creativity. "It can be difficult for people to reconcile mental illness with the idea that traits may not be disabling. While people accept that there are health benefits to anxiety, they are more wary of schizophrenia and manic depression," says Professor Gordon Claridge, emeritus professor of abnormal psychology at Oxford University, who has edited a special edition of the journal *Personality and Individual Differences*, looking at the links between mental illness and creativity. "There is now a feeling that these traits have survived because they have some adaptive value. To be mildly manic depressive or mildly schizophrenic brings a flexibility of thought, an openness, and risk-taking behaviour, which does have some adaptive value in creativity. The price paid for having those traits is that some will have mental illness."

Mild Psychopathology and Creative Ability

Research is providing support for the idea that creative people are more likely to have traits associated with mental illness. One study found that the incidence of mood disorders, suicide and institutionalisation to be 20 times higher among major British and Irish poets in the 200 years up to 1800. Other studies have shown that psychiatric patients perform better in tests of abstract thinking. Another study, based on 291 eminent and creative men in different fields, found that 69 per cent had a mental disorder of some kind. Scientists were the least affected, while artists and writers had increased diagnoses of psychosis.

"Most theorists agree that it is not the full-blown illness itself, but the milder forms of psychosis that are at the root of the association between creativity and madness," says Emilie Glazer, experimental psychologist and author of one of the Oxford journal papers. "The underlying traits linked with mild psychopathology enhance creative ability. In severe form, they are debilitating."

Research is also showing that traits associated with different mental illnesses have different effects on creativity. The

Should Mild Mental Illness Be Treated?

Many artists and scientists suffering from mild mental illnesses, including [mathematician] John Nash, have refused treatment because they claim it blunted their creativity. The medical profession is therefore faced with a dilemma of deciding whether or not to insist on treatment for mild mental afflictions knowing that their treatment could stifle creativity, while untreated, a percentage of patients, especially those with bipolar disorder, might worsen and commit suicide.

Kenneth Lyen,
"Beautiful Minds:
Is There a Link Between Madness and Genius?"
SMA News, vol. 34, no.3, March 2002.

creativity needed to develop the theory of relativity, is, for example, very different from that required for producing surreal paintings, or poetry.

Research is now honing in on whether the psychosis that is linked to different types of creativity comes through schizophrenia and schizotypy traits, through manic-depressive or cyclothymic traits, or traits associated with the autism and Asperger's disorders. A study at the University of Newcastle [in Australia] found significant differences between artistically creative people and mathematicians. While the artists showed schizotypy traits, mathematicians did not, and that fits in with the idea that mathematics and engineering, which require attention to detail, are closer to the autistic traits than to psychosis.

"Affective disorder perpetuates creativity limited to the normal," says Glazer, "while the schizoid person is predisposed to a sense of detachment from the world, free from social boundaries and able to consider alternative frameworks, producing creativity within the revolutionary sphere. [Isaac] Newton and Einstein's schizotypal orientation, for instance, enabled their revolutionary stamp in the sciences."

The stereotypical images of mad scientists working alone and preferring foaming beakers to friends, abound in literature, and reflect a popular perception of the aloof, detached and obsessive genius. But the idea goes back even further. 2000 years ago in Rome, the philosopher Seneca was obviously already on the case when he wrote: "There is no great genius without a tincture of madness."

It's No Joke: Comedians and Depression

Heard the one about the man who went to the doctor to get help for his depression? He's told to go and see a show with a well-known comedian who would make him laugh and lift his spirits. "But that's me," says the patient. "I'm the comedian."

The joke, related by Rod Martin, author of *The Psychology of Humor—An Integrative Approach*, is apparently something of a favourite among comedians, who are known to be prone to depression, from the late Tony Hancock and Spike Milligan, to Stephen Fry and Paul Merton.

One theory is that humour is developed in response to depression, and that it works as a coping mechanism. One study, reported by Martin, looked at 55 male and 14 female comedians, all famous and successful. It found that comedians tended to be superior in intelligence, angry, suspicious, and depressed.

In addition, their early lives were characterised by suffering, isolation, and feelings of deprivation, and, he says, they used humour as a defence against anxiety, converting their feelings of suppressed rage from physical to verbal aggression. "The comedic skills required for a successful career may well be developed as a means of compensating for earlier psychological losses and difficulties," says Martin. A second study did not find higher levels, although comedians had significantly greater preoccupation with themes of good and evil, unworthiness, self-deprecation, and duty and responsibility.

"A significant proportion of comedians do seem to suffer more with depression," says Professor Gordon Claridge, emeritus professor of abnormal psychology at Oxford University. "Comedy seems to act as a way of dealing with depression. I think there is an emotionality and cognitive style that goes along with these depressive disorders which seems to feed creativity."

Salvador Dali was not just a great artist. He also met the criteria for several psychosis diagnoses, a mixture of schizophrenic and depressive. He may also have been paranoid, as well as having antisocial, histrionic, and narcissistic disorders. "Dali and his contribution to the history of art highlights that abnormality is not necessarily disagreeable—or to be so readily dismissed as a sign of neurological disease. For without his instability, Dali may not have created the great art that he did," says Caroline Murphy of Oxford.

> *"There is a widespread highly romanticized belief that madness somehow heightens creative genius among artists, writers, and musicians."*

The Link Between Mental Illness and Creativity Is Misunderstood

Hara Estroff Marano

Hara Estroff Marano is editor-at-large of Psychology Today. *In the following viewpoint, Marano claims that the relationship between mental illness and creativity is widely romanticized and misunderstood. Mood disorders, she maintains, do not heighten creative genius: Realizing great ideas requires the emotional stability for hard work and discipline. Moreover, the author explains that self-reflection, struggles against poverty and public indifference, and high expectations cause artists to suffer more from emotional distress and depression.*

As you read, consider the following questions:

1. What are the two important components of "creative leaps," according to the author?

Hara Estroff Marano, "Genius and Madness," *Psychology Today*, May 7, 2007. Copyright © 2007 Sussex Publishers, Inc. Reproduced by permission.

2. What example does Marano provide to demystify the creative process?

3. What ability must truly creative people have, in the author's view?

There may be a link between creativity and mental disorders, but it is probably not in the way that you think. There is a widespread highly romanticized belief that madness somehow heightens creative genius among artists, writers, and musicians. And that may be because we romanticize the idea of artistic inspiration.

As with mental disorders, there is something mysterious and unexplainable about the creative process. But all significant creative leaps have two very important components—talent and technique. By far the most universal and necessary aspect of technique is dogged persistence, which is anything but romantic.

Psychologist Mihaly Csikszentmihalyi, best known for his work on flow, has spent four decades studying the creative process. He recounts the experience of sculptor Nina Holton. "Tell anybody you're a sculptor and they'll say, 'Oh, how exciting, how wonderful,'" Holton told him. Her response to such comments: "What's so wonderful?" Then she explains that being a sculptor is "like being a mason or a carpenter half the time." She finds that "they don't wish to hear that because they really only imagine the first part, the exciting part. But, as Khrushchev once said, that doesn't fry pancakes, you see. That germ of an idea does not make a sculpture that stands up. So the next stage is the hard work. Can you really translate it into a piece of sculpture?"

Even acknowledged creative geniuses find that endurance must follow intuition. [Albert] Einstein's ideas were not worked out in a day. It takes a great deal of discipline, and often many bouts of trial and error, to work out an idea. Follow-through is critical to the realization of an idea. Discipline is

Mental Illness Inhibits Creativity

Indeed, outright psychopathology usually inhibits rather than helps creative expression. Even more significant is the fact that a very large proportion of creators exhibit no pathological symptoms, at least not to any measurable degree. Hence, psychopathology is by no means a sine qua non [essential element] of creativity. Instead, it is probably more accurate to say that creativity shares certain cognitive and dispositional traits with specific symptoms, and that the degree of that commonality is contingent on the level and type of creativity that an individual displays.

Dean Keith Simonton, "Are Genius and Madness Related? Contemporary Answers to an Ancient Question," Psychiatric Times, May 31, 2005.

not a hallmark of minds in the throes of emotional distress. "Despite the carefree air that many creative people effect," says Csikszentmihalyi, "most of them work late into the night and persist when less driven individuals would not."

Even having ideas can take a great deal of discipline. Robert Root-Bernstein is another longtime observer of the creative process. "If the writer doesn't sit at the computer every day," he points out. "The muse is not going to visit."

The Consequences of the Creative Lifestyle

Nevertheless, some forms of emotional distress are more common among writers, artists and musicians. Serious depression strikes artists ten times more often than it does the general population. The link, however, is not creativity. Artists are more likely to be self-reflective and to ruminate, to mull things over. And that thinking style—as opposed to creativity it-self—is a hallmark of depression and commonly leads to it.

Evidence that madness does nothing to heighten creative genius comes from a study done by psychologist Robert Weisberg. He studied in detail the creative output, along with the letters and medical records, of composer Robert Schumann, who was known to endure bouts of manic depression that drove him to attempt suicide.

Indeed, Schumann wrote a great deal of music during his manic intervals. But quantity is one thing and quality is another. Truly creative people are not just capable of producing novelty; they must have the ability to tell a good idea from a bad idea. Weisberg found that Schumann's compositional output indeed swelled during his manic years, but the average quality of his efforts did not change. To judge compositional caliber, Weisberg relied on an objective measure: the number of recordings available of a given work.

When mania struck, Schumann wrote more great pieces—but he also turned out more ordinary ones, too. Mania "jacks up the energy level," Weisberg points out, "but it doesn't give the person access to ideas that he or she wouldn't have had otherwise."

It's entirely possible, Weisberg notes, that the elevated rates of mental disorders among artistic geniuses come about as a result of the creative lifestyle, which hardly provides emotional stability. Many artists struggle against poverty and public indifference in their lifetime. And if they do indeed produce works that are acclaimed, they could succumb to the overwhelming pressure to live up to their earlier successes.

What's more, says Csikszentmihalyi, the openness and sensitivity of creative people can expose them to suffering and pain. As electrical engineer Jacob Rabinow told him, "Inventors have a low threshold of pain. Things bother them." And yet, few things in life bring more satisfaction and fulfillment than the process of creation.

Periodical and Internet Sources Bibliography

The following articles have been selected to supplement the diverse views presented in this chapter.

Peter Ford	"In Modern China, Eye on Mental Health," *Christian Science Monitor*, November 13, 2007.
Elizabeth King Humphrey	"The Mad Artist's Brain: The Connection Between Creativity and Mental Illness," *Scientific American*, November 22, 2010.
Ferris Jabr	"Self-Fulfilling Fakery: Feigning Mental Illness Is a Form of Self-Deception," *Scientific American*, July 28, 2010.
Gary G. Kohls	"America's Mental Illness Epidemic: It Turns Out That the Drugs Are the Problem," *Online Journal*, August 26, 2010.
Christopher Lane	"Bitterness: The Next Mental Disorder?" *Psychology Today*, May 28, 2009.
Jonah Lehrer	"Depression's Upside," *New York Times*, February 25, 2010.
Bruce E. Levine	"The Astonishing Rise of Mental Illness in America," CounterPunch, April 28, 2010. www.counterpunch.org.
Rick Nauert	"Medical Care Lags for Mentally Ill," PsychCentral, October 17, 2007. http://psychcentral.com.
Carolyn Robinowitz	"Reports of Our Death Have Been Greatly Exaggerated," *Psychiatric News*, September 7, 2007.
Adrienne Sussman	"Mental Illness and Creativity: A Neurological View of the 'Tortured Artist,'" *Stanford Journal of Neuroscience*, Fall 2007.

OPPOSING VIEWPOINTS® SERIES

CHAPTER 2

How Should Society Address Mental Illness?

Chapter Preface

On January 8, 2011, a shooting at a public meeting near a supermarket in Tucson, Arizona, left six people dead and fourteen injured, including US Representative Gabrielle Giffords, who survived a close-range gunshot to the head. The primary suspect, Jared Lee Loughner, was described as a "political radical" and "loner" by a friend, according to a January 9, 2011, article by Jon Swaine in the *Telegraph*. According to the same article, a former classmate at Pima Community College claimed that the twenty-two-year-old Loughner was "obviously disturbed" and interrupted class with "nonsensical outbursts." After ranting that the college was illegal under the Constitution in a YouTube video, Loughner dropped out in October 2010 after refusing to attain clearance from a mental health professional that he did not pose a danger to himself and those around him. In another YouTube video, posted on December 15, 2010, Loughner wrote, "The government is implying mind control and brainwash on the people by controlling grammar."

Loughner's personal history revived the debate surrounding statutes like Kendra's Law, the controversial New York law that permits the courts to commit individuals to treatment if they exhibit threatening behavior and refuse therapy. "If they do not comply with the court-ordered treatment plan, they can and should be involuntarily admitted to a hospital," maintains E. Fuller Torrey, founder of the Treatment Advocacy Center, in a January 12, 2011, article in the *Wall Street Journal*. "Arizona has such a provision in its laws, but it is almost never used." Reports that emerged after the shooting, Torrey points out, indicate that Loughner showed signs of untreated schizophrenia, such as "delusional ideas" and "incoherent thought processes." Nonetheless, others comment that determining who presents a real risk to the community can be problematic. "The line is extremely hard to draw in practice," according to Harvey Silverglate, an attorney and cofounder of Foundation for Individual Rights in Education quoted in a January 12, 2011, Reuters article. In the following chapter, the authors deliberate the policies regarding the treatment of mental illnesses and the legal rights and treatment needs of those who suffer from them.

| "Schizophrenia and manic-depressive ill-
ness can severely impair an individual's
self-awareness, causing many to believe
they are healthy and not in need of
medical care."

Involuntary Treatment Is Warranted for the Severely Mentally Ill

Treatment Advocacy Center

Based in Arlington, Virginia, Treatment Advocacy Center (TAC) is a nonprofit organization aimed at improving access to psychiatric treatment. In the following viewpoint, TAC contends that assisted outpatient treatment (or involuntary outpatient commitment) is a tool for the courts and families to assist the mentally ill who do not realize they are sick and present risks to themselves and others. Most recipients of assisted outpatient treatment report great improvements in health and adherence to treatment, TAC claims. TAC also points out that these programs dramatically cut the rates of homelessness, institutionalization, arrest, and incarceration among the mentally ill.

As you read, consider the following questions:

1. What is TAC's position on assisted outpatient treatment and civil rights?

2. Why does TAC maintain that greater access to assisted outpatient treatment is needed?

3. How does TAC respond to the concern that assisted outpatient treatment will fill hospitals with the mentally ill?

What is assisted outpatient treatment?

Assisted outpatient treatment [AOT] (also called things like involuntary outpatient commitment or mandated community treatment) promotes availability and accessibility for those that are most at risk. It allows the courts to order outpatient treatment for people with severe mental illnesses who are least able to help themselves or most likely to present a risk to others, giving family members and the mental health community a tool to help very sick people who cannot make their own medical decisions. At least 40% of the 4.5 million people in the United States who are diagnosed with either schizophrenia or manic depression, the two severest forms of mental illness, do not and cannot realize they are sick because the illness affects their brain's frontal-lobe function, which is necessary to make that determination. Because they do not know they are sick, they refuse medication and often deteriorate. Assisted outpatient treatment commits the patient to the treatment system, but it also commits the treatment system to the patient.

Does assisted outpatient treatment take away someone's civil rights?

No. It is the illness, not the treatment, that restricts civil liberties. Medicines can free individuals from the prison of their psychosis and enable them to engage in a meaningful exercise of their civil liberties. Assisted outpatient treatment cuts the need for incarceration, restraints, and involuntary inpatient commitment, allowing individuals to retain more of their civil liberties.

Assisted Outpatient Treatment Is Overwhelmingly Endorsed

What do people who have been helped through assisted treatment think about AOT?

There are a variety of viewpoints within the consumer community. Some consumers oppose assisted treatment. Others support assisted treatment. The Treatment Advocacy Center has consumers on its board and staff and in its membership, all of whom support wider use of this valuable treatment mechanism. A study reported in the February 7, 1997, issue of *Psychiatric News* of forcibly treated, discharged psychiatric patients found that 60 percent retrospectively favored having been treated against their will.

The most compelling argument for assisted outpatient treatment comes from those consumers who've actually participated in an AOT program. Researchers with the New York State Psychiatric Institute and Columbia University conducted face-to-face interviews with AOT recipients in New York to assess their opinions about the program, perceptions of coercion or stigma associated with the court order and, most importantly, quality of life as a result of AOT. While the interviews showed that the experience of being court-ordered into treatment made about half of recipients feel angry or embarrassed, after they received treatment, AOT recipients overwhelmingly endorsed the effect of the program on their lives:

- 75 percent reported that AOT helped them gain control over their lives;

- 81 percent said that AOT helped them to get and stay well; and

- 90 percent said AOT made them more likely to keep appointments and take medication.

Additionally, 87 percent said they were confident in their case manager's ability to help them; and 88 percent said that they and their case manager agreed on what is important for them to work on.

Which states have laws supporting assisted outpatient treatment?

Every state has a law supporting assisted outpatient treatment except for six—Connecticut, Maryland, Massachusetts, Nevada, New Mexico, and Tennessee. . . .

Do the states that have AOT use it?

No, all states with AOT laws do not use them. Often this stems from lack of education or misinformation; sometimes because of the way a law is written it is difficult to use.

Assisted Outpatient Treatment Has Proven Successful

Does assisted outpatient treatment work?

Yes.

Studies and experiences in Arizona, Hawaii, Iowa, New York, North Carolina, and other states have definitively proven assisted outpatient treatment works. For example, in New York, during the course of court-ordered treatment when compared to the three years prior to participation in the program, AOT recipients experienced far less hospitalization, homelessness, arrest, and incarceration. Specifically, of those in the AOT program:

- 74 percent fewer experienced homelessness;

- 77 percent fewer experienced psychiatric hospitalization;

- 83 percent fewer experienced arrest; and

- 87 percent fewer experienced incarceration.

Less Restrictive Treatment Alternatives

A generation ago, civil commitments to state mental hospitals were best measured in months or years. Assisted outpatient treatment has helped change that expectation. Assisted outpatient treatment . . . permits a mentally ill person to be treated in a much less restrictive environment than a state hospital while still allowing judicial monitoring of the administration of the person's treatment plan.

Randy T. Rogers and Jonathan Stanley,
"Assisted Outpatient Treatment: 'A Step in the Right Direction,'"
May 12, 2004. www.butlercountyprobatecourt.org.

Why don't people with severe mental illnesses get treatment in psychiatric facilities?

Beginning in 1955 with the widespread introduction of the first, effective antipsychotic medication chlorpromazine, or Thorazine, the stage was set for moving patients out of hospital settings. The pace of deinstitutionalization accelerated significantly following the enactment of Medicaid and Medicare a decade later. There was a wholesale emptying of state psychiatric hospitals in the mid-1960s and another wave of discharges in the early 1990s. Few beds remain, the waiting lists are long—that is why we need another solution for people who are able to receive treatment on an outpatient basis.

Will assisted outpatient treatment fill up hospitals with people with mental illness?

No. Assisted outpatient treatment is designed to help people function successfully out of the hospital. It helps those with a history of noncompliance with medications to adhere to a treatment plan and helps prevent them from decompensating and becoming rehospitalized. For example, participants in New York's AOT program, Kendra's Law, experienced a 77 percent decrease in psychiatric hospitalizations while in the program, as compared to the three years prior to AOT. In a North Carolina study, long-term AOT combined with routine outpatient services (three or more outpatient visits per month) reduced hospital admissions by 57 percent and length of hospital stay by 20 days compared to individuals without court-ordered treatment. The results were even more dramatic for individuals with schizophrenia and other psychotic disorders for whom long-term AOT reduced hospital admissions by 72 percent and length of hospital stay by 28 days compared to individuals without court-ordered treatment.

Will assisted outpatient treatment put more people with severe mental illness on the streets?

No. Inpatient hospitalization will still be needed for those incapable of surviving safely in the community. Assisted outpatient treatment facilitates early short-term rehospitalization for those noncompliant and likely to become dangerous.

Costs, the Constitution, and Lack of Treatment

Is assisted outpatient treatment expensive?

Assisted treatment is not expensive because it does not mandate any services that individuals with brain disorders are not already entitled to (example: case management, medications, rehabilitation). Assisted outpatient treatment orders merely require the system to facilitate compliance for noncompliant individuals by giving them the services they need to keep well and the surrounding community safe. Individuals subject to assisted treatment orders rarely violate the orders and hence interventions are infrequent. The data are also clear that the savings in hospital costs, forensic costs and other costs far offset any incremental cost of assisted treatment.

In an article in *Schizophrenia Bulletin*, Dr. Peter Weiden and Dr. Mark Olfson calculated that nationwide, over two years, the direct costs of rehospitalization attributable to neuroleptic [antipsychotic] noncompliance is approximately $700 million with $370 million for the first year and $335 million for the second. By increasing compliance, assisted outpatient treatment can generate savings that could be reinvested in the community.

Is assisted outpatient treatment constitutional?

Yes. Forty-four states and the District of Columbia have assisted outpatient treatment laws—some almost 20 years old. The U.S. Supreme Court has not overturned any of these laws.

At the state level AOT laws have been upheld wherever challenged. For instance, Kendra's Law in New York has been upheld through a series of challenges. With the latest ruling *In the Matter of K.L.*, a total of twelve judges in New York have examined the constitutionality of Kendra's Law; each of them has found the law constitutional, including the state's highest-ranking ones.

Why do so many people with severe mental illnesses go untreated?

The primary reasons for lack of treatment are threefold.

- Schizophrenia and manic-depressive illness can severely impair an individual's self-awareness, causing many to believe they are healthy and not in need of medical care. Their brain disease has impaired their brain function, and since they do not think they are sick, many of them do not actively seek treatment and often refuse it. The neurological term for this is "anosognosia," derived from the Greek for "loss of knowledge."

- Civil rights advocates have changed state laws and practices to such an extent that it is now virtually impossible to treat such individuals unless they first commit a violent act.

- Public psychiatric services have deteriorated significantly in recent years with the closure of state psychiatric hospitals. While these much-needed hospital beds have been eliminated, there has been no increase in outpatient services. In addition, the failure of for-profit managed care companies to provide services to these individuals who need them most has only further exacerbated the situation.

| "Involuntary mental health treatment is
a serious curtailment of liberty."

Involuntary Psychiatric Treatment Violates Patients' Rights to Autonomy

Mental Health America

Formerly known as the National Mental Health Association, Mental Health America (MHA) is a nonprofit advocacy group based in Alexandria, Virginia. In the following viewpoint, MHA contends that most patients with mental disorders are competent enough to make their own health care decisions. The group states that court-ordered treatments—whether for hospitalization, involuntary medication, or treatments conditional for parole—should only be used as a last resort, with strict safeguards, and under fair and regular review. Psychiatric treatment and services, MHA claims, are most effective when voluntary.

As you read, consider the following questions:

1. What procedural protections must be in place, according to MHA?

2. What is MHA's stance on the qualified right to refuse treatment?

3. Why does MHA oppose outpatient commitment?

Mental Health America (MHA) believes that effective protection of human rights and the best hope for recovery from mental illness comes from access to voluntary mental health treatment and services that are comprehensive, community-based, recovery-oriented and culturally and linguistically competent. Moreover, the rights of persons with mental health conditions to make decisions concerning their treatment must be respected. MHA urges states to adopt laws that reflect a commitment to maximizing the dignity, autonomy and self-determination of persons affected by mental health conditions. Voluntary admissions to treatment and services should be made more truly voluntary, and the use of advance directives should be implemented.

Specifically, Mental Health America believes that involuntary treatment in an inpatient setting should only occur as a last resort and should be limited to instances where persons pose a serious risk of physical harm to themselves or others and to circumstances when no less restrictive alternatives will respond adequately to the risk. For involuntary treatment to be used, stringent procedural safeguards and fair and regular reviews are essential.

Background

Persons with mental health conditions deserve the same degree of personal autonomy as other citizens with disabilities when it comes to receiving services. This has not always been the case. For years, persons with mental health conditions have been combating the centuries-old stereotype that they are not competent enough to make their own decisions, or to be in charge of their own mental health care. Today, we know otherwise that persons with mental health conditions are not only capable of making their own decisions regarding their care, but that mental health treatment and services can only be effective when the consumer embraces it, not when it is coercive and involuntary. Involuntary mental health treatment is a serious curtailment of liberty.

Involuntary mental health treatment occurs in a variety of contexts. The most common type of involuntary mental health treatment is court-ordered commitment to an inpatient mental health facility. However, involuntary treatment also includes involuntary medication or other treatments including electroconvulsive therapy, whether court-ordered or imposed by mental health professionals, treatment imposed upon persons with mental health conditions in prisons and jails or as a condition of probation, supervision or parole, outpatient commitment, and the use of guardianship or conservatorship laws. While MHA recognizes that involuntary treatment may sometimes be necessary, we do not support the use of involuntary outpatient treatment.

Principles and Understandings

Mental Health America recognizes that there are limited circumstances when involuntary commitment must be used as a last resort. Even in such circumstances, MHA believes that involuntary treatment is only appropriate for a very small subset of people. When involuntary treatment is used, it must be based on the following principles and understandings which are designed to ensure that the rights of persons with mental health conditions are protected:

I. Presumption of Competency. A basic principle of law in the United States is that all adults are presumed to be "competent"—that is, they are presumed to be capable of making their own decisions about their own lives and their own medical care, including mental health treatment.

II. Declaration of Incompetency. Every state has court procedures for determining when and if someone is incompetent. Only a tiny percentage of persons with mental health conditions have ever been declared incompetent under these procedures. This corresponds with the reality that almost all persons with even the most serious mental illnesses are competent most of the time—that is, they are capable of making their own decisions about whether to seek treatment and support and what treatment and support they should receive.

III. Informed Consent. Informed consent is required for all medical care provided to persons who are competent. Unless and until a person has been declared to be incompetent, informed consent is required when mental health services are provided.

IV. Standard: Serious Risk of Physical Harm to Themselves or Others in the Near Future. Involuntary commitment to a mental hospital should be limited to persons who pose a serious risk of physical harm to themselves or others in the near future. Under no circumstances should involuntary commitment be imposed upon someone based upon a risk of harm to property or a risk of nonphysical harm.

V. Least Restrictive Alternative. Persons with mental health conditions can and should be treated in the least restrictive environment and in a manner designed to preserve their dignity and autonomy and to maximize the opportunities for recovery.

VI. Procedural Protections. Persons facing involuntary confinement have a right to substantial procedural protections. Those protections should include:

A. A judicial hearing at which at least one mental health professional is required to testify

B. The right to be represented by competent counsel, including appointed counsel if indigent

C. An independent mental health evaluation

D. The right to appeal an adverse decision, including the appointment of appellate counsel and waiver of appellate costs if indigent

E. Short time limits on any commitment or procedures for regular review of continued confinement which are either automatic or readily accessible to persons with serious mental illnesses confined in a hospital

F. Involuntary commitment to a psychiatric hospital should only be imposed if supported by clear and convincing evidence. *Addington v. Texas*, 441 U.S. 418 (1979)

VII. Qualified Right to Refuse Treatment. There are a growing number of effective treatments for mental health conditions, including psychotropic medications. However, all medications pose some risks and many pose quite serious risks to the health of the persons who take them, particularly when medications are taken for extended periods to treat chronic illnesses. For this reason and because of its commitment to the autonomy and dignity of persons with mental health conditions, MHA strongly agrees with the judgment of the United States Supreme Court that all persons, even persons lawfully convicted and serving a sentence of imprisonment, have a right to refuse medication and that medication may not be imposed involuntarily unless rigorous standards and procedures are met. *Washington v. Harper*, 494 U.S.210 (1990).

Protecting Autonomy

VIII. Opposition to Outpatient Treatment. MHA is opposed to outpatient commitment. Outpatient commitment has not been shown to be effective in reducing hospitalization or other adverse outcomes. Studies have repeatedly shown that when persons with even the most serious mental illnesses are provided with appropriate and comprehensive community mental health services, they succeed. Mandatory treatment has not been shown to add to the effectiveness of community mental health services and, indeed, may interfere with recovery by compromising personal responsibility and lowering self-esteem.

A Pessimistic View of Patients' Prognosis

Assisted, or coerced, outpatient treatment, has at its core a much more pessimistic view—that illness will continue to a degree that will require coercion for an extended period. Psychiatrists are certainly very aware of the often chronic nature of the illnesses in our patients. We are very aware that our goal must be to help empower our patients to live as full a life as possible, and that what constitutes a full life must be as seen by the patient. Clearly there are many times when our patients chose to live very differently, but the principle of autonomy demands that we respect this, unless there is very compelling reason to intervene.

Kenneth Certa,
"Testimony of Kenneth Certa, MD, DFAPA,
on Behalf of the Pennsylvania Psychiatric Society,
Before the Senate Public Health and Welfare Committee,
Regarding Senate Bill 226 (Mental Heath Procedures Act:
Assisted Community Treatment)," October 2, 2007.
www.senatorerickson.com.

While MHA does not support involuntary outpatient commitment, it also recognizes that it is a reality in communities across the nation. In communities where involuntary outpatient commitment is implemented, the following principles should be adhered to in order to insure that an individual's autonomy is not diminished:

A. Under no circumstances should such an arrangement be used to lengthen the period of involuntary treatment otherwise authorized by law.

B. There should be substantial evidence that no less coercive arrangement would permit the person's safe release.

C. The need for involuntary community treatment should be based upon a significant history of highly unsuccessful community treatment despite the provision of comprehensive community supports.

D. The person's failure to comply with an involuntary treatment order in the community should not, standing alone, be the basis for revocation of release or re-commitment. Such revocation or recommitment should only be imposed upon persons who otherwise meet the standard for inpatient commitment—i.e., dangerousness to self or others.

IX. Voluntary Treatment Should Be Truly Voluntary. Coercion occurs during many so-called "voluntary" admissions. *Zinermon v. Burch,* 494 U.S. 113 (1990). Persons facing involuntary commitment are routinely offered the option of becoming voluntary patients. However, in many treatment facilities, a person who has been voluntarily admitted is not free to leave when she or he chooses. Rather, it is common for mental health laws to permit the facility to detain a person for up to one week after she or he indicates a desire to leave. MHA urges states to eliminate this form of admission and admit persons to mental health facilities in the same manner as persons are admitted to medical treatment facilities for nonpsychiatric illnesses.

X. Advance Directives. Advance directives have proven to be useful instruments for maintaining and increasing the autonomy of persons with mental health conditions. MHA urges states to create and enforce laws which permit persons with mental illnesses to designate in writing, while competent, what treatment they should receive should their decisional capacity be impaired at a later date. Such laws should reflect the following principles:

A. There should be sufficient protections in place to ensure that such directives are created voluntarily and with informed consent.

B. In the absence of a judicial finding that, absent involuntary treatment, the person is dangerous to self or others, a directive refusing treatment must be honored.

C. As long as the advance directive does not conflict with accepted medical practice, the person's choice of treatment should be honored.

D. There should be clear mechanisms for creating, modifying and revoking an advance directive. . . .

MHA affiliates and other advocates should periodically examine state laws and the practices of treatment facilities and the courts, including the criminal justice and probate systems as well as the private and public mental health systems, to minimize coercion in mental health treatment wherever and whenever it occurs. Special attention needs to be paid to eliminating any discrimination against persons with mental health conditions seeking to be discharged from treatment and to legislating and advocating the use of advance directives, in which the person directs his or her own treatment.

> *"There are reasons to suspect that com-*
> *bat trauma differs from other types of*
> *events."*

Mentally Ill Veterans Need More Effective Psychotherapy

Norra MacReady

Based in Los Angeles, California, Norra MacReady has been a medical writer for more than twenty years. In the following viewpoint, she states that veterans with post-traumatic stress disorder (PTSD) face particular challenges and issues. MacReady explains that these individuals may develop worldviews, or "cognitive schemas," that the world is extremely dangerous, the self cannot minimize harm, and the self is to blame for the occurrence of trauma. Also, they suffer from more severe PTSD than civilians and often have injuries that hinder treatment, she continues. Therefore, the author recommends that comprehensive evaluations and better outreach and education programs for veterans are necessary.

Norra MacReady, "Challenges of Treating PTSD in Veterans," Medscape, November 2, 2008. Reprinted with permission from Medscape.com, 2011. Available at http://www.medscape.com/viewarticle/584096.

As you read, consider the following questions:

1. Why is cognitive behavioral therapy a questionable treatment approach for veterans, according to Dr. Rachel Yehuda?

2. How must veterans be educated about psychiatric treatment, in MacReady's opinion?

3. What is the importance of a group dynamic in treating veterans?

Veterans with post-traumatic stress disorder (PTSD) may require treatment tailored to the unique nature of combat, military culture, and their individual circumstances, Rachel Yehuda, PhD, said at the annual meeting of the US Psychiatric and Mental Health Congress.

Dr. Yehuda, professor of psychiatry and director of the Traumatic Stress Studies Division at the Mount Sinai School of Medicine in New York City, cited a review in which the authors, Foa and Meadows, suggested that people may develop certain worldviews, or "cognitive schemas," in response to the traumatic event. Those schemas state that:

- The world is overly dangerous;

- The self is incompetent to minimize damage; and

- The self is to blame for the traumatic exposure.

Some people may be predisposed to develop PTSD because "maybe the person had these schemas before the event," she said. The schemas might act as risk factors for PTSD, which is then triggered by the traumatic event. "PTSD may be associated with individual characteristics that are expressed in the presence of trauma. As a result, certain people don't deploy their natural recovery processes following trauma exposure but may develop symptoms 15 or 20 years later," Dr. Yehuda explained.

Research vs. Reality

Over the past decade, cognitive behavioral treatments (CBT) such as exposure therapy or cognitive processing therapy have become the standard of practice for PTSD with demonstrated efficacy in clinical trials. Most of these studies were conducted on women who had been victims of interpersonal violence, or men and women who had been through motor vehicle accidents or natural disasters such as earthquakes. A few studies have involved refugees. Given the nature of traumatic combat experience, "there are reasons to suspect that combat trauma differs from other types of events," Dr. Yehuda noted.

The premise of behavioral therapy is that recovery occurs through gradual repeated exposure to the situation associated with the trauma in an attempt to decrease the PTSD symptoms and subsequent avoidant behavior. For example, the survivor of a plane crash who now fears flying might start by sitting in an airplane and eventually progress to taking a short flight. Over time, the person re-habituates to the situation, and the anxiety resolves. The cognitive therapy component of treatment helps to modify the cognitive distortions developed from the traumatic event, thereby reducing the intensity of the associated emotional reaction. Often these 2 therapies (CBT) are combined for behavioral exposure with alteration of cognitive schema.

This approach may work for PTSD associated with a single or time-limited event, but has questionable value for PTSD arising from warfare, which involves repetitive and chronic exposure to combat trauma, Dr. Yehuda pointed out. In fact, there are many real-life obstacles to using CBT on people with PTSD, regardless of its cause. When in combat, soldiers are often sent back to combat after a short time so severe PTSD and avoidant behavior do not develop. However, when veterans return home, this approach would be inappropriate.

Research findings are often limited in their clinical utility because trials frequently exclude the most challenging patients, such as people who are suicidal, substance abusers, or have comorbidities. "The patients that clinicians see may be very different than those examined in clinical trials," she explained. So clinical trials offer guidance to treatment but clinicians need to decide on the most effective approach for their specific patient given individual variables.

Studies in Veterans

Several studies have examined PTSD in veterans. In 1 study, 360 Vietnam veterans with PTSD were randomized to undergo either trauma-focused group psychotherapy, or a present-centered comparison treatment that avoided focusing specifically on trauma. An intention-to-treat analysis showed no differences between the groups on any treatment outcome. Sixty veterans with chronic military-related PTSD participated in a wait-list controlled study of cognitive processing therapy (CPT). The dropout rate was 20% from the CPT group and 13% from the waiting list. At the post-treatment evaluation, 90% of the people in the CPT group either no longer met the diagnostic criteria for PTSD or experienced significant symptom improvement. Interestingly, there was no relationship between these outcomes and PTSD disability status. Similarly, the intensity of PTSD symptoms diminished among 59 Croatian veterans who participated in dynamic group psychotherapy for 5 years, but there was no change in other neurotic symptoms or defense mechanisms. Virtual reality showed promise in a study of eight Vietnam veterans exposed to a "virtual Vietnam." After 8 to 16 sessions, there was a significant reduction in symptoms compared to baseline. This effect persisted at 3 months but not at 6 months, although there was a trend toward fewer intrusive thoughts and less avoidance. In a study comparing eye movement desensitization and reprocessing (EMDR) to biofeedback and routine clinical care in the treatment of PTSD in combat veterans, EMDR was associated with a significantly greater treatment effect that was maintained at

Concerns About Elevated Rates of Suicide

Because of the high rates of mental disorders in service members returning from Afghanistan and Iraq, there are concerns about elevated rates of suicide. According to DOD [Department of Defense], the rate of suicide in the military in 2003 was comparable with the rate across all ages of the general US population (about 10 per 100,000). Since then, the Army has reported a record of over 140 suicides in active-duty soldiers in 2008; in November 2009, the Army released data suggesting that suicides in 2009 could exceed that number. In January–October 2009, there were 133 reported suicides (90 confirmed and 43 pending); in the same period in 2008, there were 115 confirmed suicides in active-duty soldiers. Those figures do not take into account the other branches of the US military, and it is not possible to determine whether the rate of suicide in all military personnel has increased. However, some data suggest that there are especially vulnerable groups, notably veterans who served in the active component and veterans who have mental disorders.

Committee on the Initial Assessment of Readjustment Needs of Military Personnel, Veterans, and Their Families, Board on the Health of Selected Populations, Institute of Medicine, Returning Home From Iraq and Afghanistan: Preliminary Assessment of Readjustment Needs of Veterans, Service Members, and Their Families. Washington, DC: The National Academies Press, 2010.

3 months. Because of the small number of subjects (10 subjects underwent EMDR, 13 received biofeedback, and 12 got routine care), Dr. Yehuda cautioned drawing definitive conclusions from this study.

Barriers to Care

Along with all of the questions about clinical trials and CBT, veterans have their own set of issues and concerns that complicate any attempts to treat PTSD, Yehuda suggested. Many of these may conspire to make veterans' treatment resistant; for example:

- Their PTSD may be more severe or chronic than the PTSD seen in civilians;

- Veterans who use Veterans Affairs (VA) hospitals may be a self-selecting group; they may differ from veterans who seek private care or simply try to tough things out on their own;

- They may have comorbidities, such as traumatic brain injuries (TBI) or other medical or psychiatric conditions that make them harder to treat. For example, some of the drugs used to treat TBI may exacerbate the symptoms of PTSD. Substance abuse may further complicate treatment; and

- The VA's own structure, which requires an extensive consent process, could be a barrier to research.

In Dr. Yehuda's opinion, the relationship between psychotherapy and pharmacotherapy requires more study. Veterans often are more open than the general public to the idea of taking medication, unfortunately, because psychotherapy is usually administered by a different clinician in the VA system, treatment fragmentation occurs. "This provides a confusing message for the veteran patient," she said.

Treatment Recommendations

Behavioral disturbances ascribed to PTSD in veterans may actually result from other causes, Dr. Yehuda warned. Clinicians should assess whether the disability results from PTSD or from a preexisting pattern of self-damaging behaviors or poor coping skills. She made the following recommendations for treating combat veterans:

- Recommend that each veteran undergo a comprehensive evaluation that includes psychosocial, vocational, interpersonal, and medical conditions, as well as psychiatric illness;

- Establish a therapeutic alliance aimed at a long-term relationship;

- Do more outreach: Veterans require more than people in conventional settings;

- Educate veterans; help them realize that treatment as soon as possible after the traumatic event is more beneficial than waiting;

- Anticipate the tendency to drop out of treatment; work with the patient to develop a plan for handling that temptation early in the treatment course; and

- Use specialized treatments judiciously.

Dr. Yehuda also emphasized the importance of the group dynamic in veterans' care. These patients often mistrust non-veterans and feel that only their fellow service people can truly understand what they have been through. "Recently returning veterans do not trust the government to fix problems they think the government caused—they have to learn that the VA is not the Department of Defense," Dr. Yehuda explained. She pointed out that many veterans are reluctant to seek mental healthcare at all, and do so only under pressure from their families. Those who do try to navigate their way through the healthcare system often find that the services available are not the ones they need. To be optimally helpful to veterans, she said, "mental health should be incorporated into the bigger picture of healthcare in a more seamless manner."

> "To call the devastating effects of war 'mental illness' is to make the colossal mistake of thinking that the problem springs solely from within the person's psyche."

Psychotherapy May Not Be Beneficial to Military Veterans

Paula J. Caplan

Paula J. Caplan is a clinical and research psychologist at Harvard University and author of They Say You're Crazy: How the World's Most Powerful Psychiatrists Decide Who's Normal. *In the following viewpoint, Caplan argues that veterans' feelings of rage, fear, or suicide are normal, human reactions to the horrors of war. Rather than suffering from mental disorders, she maintains, these men and women are held up against unrealistic standards to hide their emotions, and psychiatric treatment may not be beneficial. Therefore, Caplan advises that the emotional isolation of veterans must be countered through social support and open acknowledgment of their pain and suffering.*

As you read, consider the following questions:

1. How does the military respond to survivor's guilt, according to Caplan?

2. What is Caplan's view of treatments for post-traumatic stress disorder (PTSD)?

3. How does Caplan argue that military therapists have harmed veterans?

"I think I must be crazy," said the Iraq War vet. "At a welcome-home ceremony the city arranged, I didn't know they were going to fire ceremonial cannons. I was holding a bottle of champagne, and when they started firing, over and over and over, I went nuts! I hurled the bottle at a tree, stuck my head between my knees, and shook until it stopped. Crazy, right?"

As a psychologist, I can report that after telling me how they feel, most people end with some equivalent of, "That means I'm crazy, doesn't it?" But the veterans of the wars in Iraq and Afghanistan ask this question with an intensity that is especially disturbing, whether they speak with me in my capacity as a professional, a journalist, or just an interested citizen. The degree of their anguish and alienation from their loved ones makes it especially hard to persuade them when the word crazy does not apply to them. Their words reveal the vividness of their torment and their despair.

Julia's Story

Julia had been home for six months after the year she spent in Baghdad, where she heard half a dozen explosions every day. Since her return, not one night had brought restful sleep. She awoke every day in a state of complete exhaustion.

All her life a sociable person, Julia was stunned to be filled with rage "at friends and family who had done nothing to me" and at herself. Driving her car, she was seized by the impulse to swerve and crash into a mountain. Only digging her fingernails into her palms until they bled and yanking hunks of hair from her head kept her from making that swerve.

"Iraq was terrifying because I had no idea how to explain my feelings," Julia said. "There were all those explosions, and my regular assignment was doing pat down searches of Iraqis who might have been friends or might have been wearing explosives. If a pat had located a bomb," she explained, "before my mind registered it, I'd have been dead. And it was rough when this larger-than-life soldier we all loved died from a roadside bomb. But I keep thinking how many thousands of soldiers have gone through this and been just fine. Not a single soldier in Iraq ever told me they were scared or angry or crazy. They were sad when the big guy died, but nobody lost control."

The thought of "maybe if I kill myself, I'll stop feeling so angry and will be able to get some sleep" churned constantly through her mind. Julia considered therapy but feared "seeing a military shrink, because that could wreck my plan to retire on a nice pension when my twenty years in the Army National Guard are up." Julia's family never had much money. "If I tell an Army therapist all this crazy shit, they'll kick me out."

Private therapists are expensive, but for six weeks, Julia saw "a very nice psychologist" and talked about her emotional numbness, which alternated between rage and despair. The therapist encouraged her to let her guard down. But Julia clung to the numbness, believing it protected people from her irrational anger. She also thought, "If I'm redeployed, I can't have my feelings exploding all the time."

Military Ethos Encourages Denial and Detachment

Military ethos discourages soldiers from talking about their fear, frustration, helplessness, and uncertainty about the progress of the war. Julia only once told someone about her feelings. While doing pat searches, she had said to a soldier, "Any of those people could kill us." He responded, "Aw, no, they won't!" Never again did she say anything less than gung-ho about her work. In no official or unofficial instruction did her sergeant or commanding officer say these reactions were normal. Someone would occasionally say that anyone who felt depressed or anxious should tell their squad leader who would send that person to a chaplain or counselor, but the nonverbal message was that needing help was unsoldierly. For the men, it was unmanly. For the women, it proved that women should not be soldiers.

Officially, the military recognizes that going to war can be upsetting. But for the most part, they have not found solutions to its resulting emotional carnage. Their top priority is to produce soldiers who, above all, continue to function. During World War II, when a soldier broke down after seeing his buddy blown to bits, the armed services usually sent him far from combat and gave him time to recuperate. In recent years, asserting the importance of protecting soldiers from "survivor guilt," they switched to the PIE approach: proximity, immediacy, and expectation. In practice, this means keeping soldiers in proximity to the combat zone when they are overwhelmed by war's horrors; getting them back to the combat zone immediately, perhaps after a few days' rest; and conveying the expectation that they will soon be fine. Of course, soldiers sent back are even more likely to see still more comrades die, thus increasing the chances they will have survivor guilt.

Often, antidepressants are handed out liberally to soldiers. Yes, the pills can distance the soldiers from their feelings. But those feelings do not vanish, and if they don't come out immediately, they will later.

Transition times are excruciating, according to Ray, a vet who flew home on a two-week leave after being holed up near Kabul for six months. In preparation for leave, he was called to a one-hour group meeting where the soldiers were told not to hit their wives. (No parallel instruction was given to women soldiers.) Ray says, "That's all the advice we got." When he landed in his small hometown, everyone asked, "What's it like over there?" Ray was dumbfounded. How could he possibly convey to the citizens of this peaceful, Midwestern place what he had seen? The power of the warlords, the constant, battering uncertainty about friends and enemies and the life-and-death stakes of a wrong guess. Even if he could convey it, *should* he? "Soldiers have a duty to protect folks back home by fighting wars abroad but also to protect them from our emotional nightmares," he said. People thought Ray was weird because he wouldn't speak when asked about the war. Chasms grew. His best friend stopped calling. Family interactions were awkward.

Julia was grateful that emotional numbness made it so much easier to protect her loved ones from both the horrors of the war and the dangers she felt within herself. She stopped going to therapy, partly because she wanted to remain numb and partly because she needed to feel like her old self. "I've always been independent and strong and I thought, 'I don't need a shrink. I can do this myself.'" But do what? She didn't know where to begin.

A college professor invited Julia to speak to her class. The previous year, home from Iraq on a brief leave, she had spouted what she now calls "the Army's book, what they want you to say." This year was different. Though trying to stay calm, she spoke freely about what she had seen, the sleep that brought no rest, the numbness. She described the self-hatred she felt when watching a TV series about the war and seeing a character handle a situation better than she had. One student asked why she was so hard on herself and why she liked staying numb. Struck by the student's compassion and the directness of the question, Julia felt it was time to tell the whole truth. "I feel like if I kill myself, maybe I can get some sleep." That night, she slept soundly for the first time in months.

What made the difference? Someone, a virtual stranger, had wanted to understand, and twenty other students were also present, listening. It was easier to talk to strangers than to the loved ones she felt more responsible to protect.

Behind Closed Doors

In our culture, we send traumatized people behind the closed doors of therapists to seek help that presumably only experts can provide. And, after all, who else really wants to hear about the real horrors of war? It's easier all around if we send vets to professionals, asking them to close the door behind them. In this way, we avoid the emotional carnage of war. But is that healthy for the vets or for us?

Good therapists can help. But soldiers and vets have been held to impossible standards of concealment of deeply human, natural feelings, and sending them to therapists carries the message that they are mentally ill, that they should be "over it" by now. And although post-traumatic stress disorder [PTSD] accurately implies that their anguish results from trauma, PTSD is located in the official listing of mental disorders, thus branding their response to war as abnormal and marginalizing them even more than the war experiences have. Furthermore, decades of experience with veterans from Vietnam and the first Gulf War indicate that providing psychotherapy and/or drugs may help, but that the suffering of many persists, wreaking havoc with relationships and jobs and often leading to addictions and eventually homelessness.

Every American can help. We can tell vets that it's not crazy to feel rage, despair, self-hatred, and self-doubt in response to being helpless in the face of constant danger, ambiguity, and ever-changing explanations of why Americans are in Iraq, of trying to match a John Wayne [an actor known for portraying "tough guy" characters] image that even John Wayne never matched in real life. If vets' emotions about those circumstances are signs of mental illness, then what, exactly, would be a healthy, human response? In his new book, *What Really Matters*, Harvard University psychiatrist and anthropologist Arthur Kleinman proposes that what we should ask is how someone could *not* have such feelings, a question that is all the more important the greater the deception and doublespeak involved—as in the wars in Iraq and Afghanistan—in the initiation and prosecution of the war.

On September 11, 2001, Drew went straight from high school to enlist in the military, consumed with avenging all those deaths and defending his country. What he had not counted on was the part of basic training when they order you to run around a field aiming a gun, yelling "Kill! Kill!" Horrified, he became obsessed with images of suicide. Compared to the thought of killing "the enemy," he found it easier to think of killing himself. One night, the pull toward suicide became so powerful that he panicked, went AWOL [absent without official leave], and flew home. The military court-martials for such conduct, but Professor Kleinman would say that Drew was exhibiting moral, caring behavior. If this is a humane world, then it is important to feel fear and horror about violence. *Not* to feel such emotions, Kleinman says, is to have a moral disorder.

True Psychopathology

A psychologist who is asked to assess a person who compulsively lies, whose lies repeatedly lead to devastation and death, and who appears to feel no remorse about the lying or its consequences will readily diagnose that person as a psychopath. It should be obvious that [former US president] George W. Bush, [former vice president] Dick Cheney, [former secretary of defense] Donald Rumsfeld, and their cronies fit that description, that that is where the true psychopathology lies, although the scale of their misconduct actually leaves psychopathology in the dust and leaps to the realm of evil. The same goes for the psychologist who is asked to assess a person who repeatedly claims that X is true; when it is patently obvious that X is false (e.g., "We're bringing democracy to the Middle East," or "They love us over there"). The psychologist would likely conclude that the person is out of touch with reality to the point of psychosis. When arrogance or greed impel the distortion of reality, rather than cognitive or emotional factors beyond the person's control, it makes more sense to call it not mental illness but villainy.

War can transform a soldier into someone they have never been and never thought they'd be. Think what it would do to most of us to live for a year in constant mortal danger with no real way to protect oneself or one's comrades; to hear many times a day the sounds that signal the deaths of other living beings, many of them your fellow citizens, and to know that these might be the sounds of your own death. If you have always had a nurturant nature, a sociable character, a peaceful soul, what happens to your sense of identity when you are expected to relish the order "Kill! Kill!"? No matter how you feel about "the enemy," at what cost does one forget that that enemy is composed of human beings?

The war is all the more crazy-making for the many soldiers who joined up for reasons other than the wish to overpower and to kill, like the ones who told me they signed on right after September 11, 2001, because they wanted to protect their country. These then-seventeen-year-olds imagined that they would be guarding airports and harbors, checking for explosives, or perhaps learning codes to work in the intelligence sphere to spot and head off attacks on the United States. Others joined the reserves or the National Guard when this country was not at war because they were too poor to pay for college or job training, and the reserves or the Guard gave them these opportunities. And every soldier who told me they signed up while in or soon after high school was devastated to learn that their recruiter blatantly lied to them, assuring them that they would never see combat and that they would have the job opportunities they most desired.

Going AWOL

When soldiers come smack up against the realities of war, turning to military therapists for help may be useful for some but has compounded the damage and danger for others. One young man who later went AWOL said a military psychiatrist reviled him for wanting out of the service, called him a coward, and said he could be locked up for a long time for trying to fake a mental illness in order to get out. Of the many soldiers I have interviewed who went AWOL, every one described first their struggle with shame and self-blame, thinking they must be overly sensitive to the military's obsession with violence and the frequent humiliation of those who are less than gung-ho about it, and feeling viscerally the emotional and sometimes physical dangers of speaking within the military about the lies and hypocrisy of these wars. For soldiers to overcome the lifelong indoctrination—intensified in basic training—of the belief that America does no wrong is a monumental task, especially after being told that they face life terms in military prisons if they try to leave. "When my Sergeant told me that's what would happen, I believed him," Drew told me. Not until he went AWOL and, months later, having hidden in a relative's home in almost total isolation and fear, happened across the American Friends Service [Committee]'s GI Rights hotline, was he on the way to learning that the sergeant had misinformed him.

The truth that soldiers know about going AWOL is that the military contacts civilian police forces with the names of those who are AWOL and instructions to pick them up on sight and return them to their bases. Describing a close call he had when a policeman rang the doorbell of the place where he was in hiding, Drew's terror was palpable, even though he has been officially discharged from the Army for months. The purposeful terrorizing of soldiers who hate these wars and want to leave the military keeps many of them on their bases until, as many have told me, for the first time in their life they have massive panic attacks or, often, consider suicide. Drew was off the base at a sandwich shop when his first panic attack hit. He was headed for Iraq within days. He said that nothing in his [past]—not his parents' divorce, not major personal problems with which he had grappled—had ever made him think of killing himself, but at that moment, he knew that suicide was the only alternative to the path he took: He walked out of the shop, hailed a taxi, flew home, and went into hiding.

Then there is Neal Howland, who was promised training as a videographer, only to learn when it was too late that he was headed for Iraq and that his job would keep him in combat zones, repairing exploded vehicles. Neal began to have vivid images of driving a car into a tree, hoping to be so maimed that he would be discharged. Only when those images became nearly irresistible did he go AWOL. Why hadn't he left before? Because the military psychologist he saw had told him that "faking a mental illness" would likely lead to court-martial and a long incarceration that would keep him from home, family, and friends until his hair turned grey.

Despite such attempts at intimidation, it appears that the phenomenon of going AWOL is more extensive than most people realize. When Neal turned himself in at Fort Knox, one of the two soldiers guarding the gate as he approached asked why he had come. After Neal said, "I've been AWOL, and, I'm turning myself in," that guard turned to his fellow and said, "We got another one!" And in the one week that Neal was there, he met more than fifty soldiers who had come to Knox for the same reason. According to Pentagon figures, more than 28,000 soldiers "deserted" between the beginning of 2002 (the war in Afghanistan began the previous autumn) and the end of 2006.

Toward Connection and Personhood

To call the devastating effects of war "mental illness" is to make the colossal mistake of thinking that the problem springs solely from within the person's psyche. Individuals vary in how they react to horror, but it would be absurd to think that everyone traumatized by war was mentally ill, rather than understandably devastated. Are Ray and Drew mentally ill? No, they're just compassionate. Are Julia and Neal masochists, who, unlike the rest of us, *enjoy* suffering? No, they want what we all want: life, safety, and tranquility.

If we ignore vets' numbness and silence, helping them to protect us, who then will protect them? Connection with and care from one's community have enormous power to heal. A wealth of research shows that social support is often the *most* important factor in emotional healing. Better still, it heals without adding to the sufferer's burden the shame of being considered crazy. We need to decrease vets' emotional isolation by creating opportunities for plentiful human interactions that will remind them that they are more than the sum of their reactions to war, thus reminding them of who they were and who they still can be.

What helped Julia, Ray, Drew, and Neal can help other vets while also helping heal a country divided by these wars. Without discouraging them from also seeking professional help, we all can offer vets a chance to speak their truth to us, to tell them that, for as long as they want to talk, we will listen. We can say that we would have reacted the same if we had been there. Just hearing those words can bring a person back toward connection and personhood and can broaden their repertoire of ways to cope. Disconnection and fear of being insane are major risk factors for severe depression and unbridled rage against oneself and others. To tell vets that we are open to hearing the horrors and shame that plague them is to take some of that poison away, to take what they have seen and felt out of the realm of "too awful to be spoken, except to a therapist who is used to craziness." We can say that as citizens of this country and as human beings, we take seriously our obligation to help veterans reconnect with those who were lucky enough to have escaped deployment, to help them back to a place of greater physical and emotional safety than perhaps they ever hoped to find again. And in reaching out to these vets, we learn and teach others the full measure of the devastation wrought by war and therefore make it less likely that, as a nation, we will go to war quickly and unthinkingly again.

All vets' names in the article have been changed to protect their privacy, with the exception of Neal Howland, who gave his permission to use his name and photographs.

Periodical and Internet Sources Bibliography

The following articles have been selected to supplement the diverse views presented in this chapter.

Boston Globe	"Protect Mental-Health Parity, but Scrutiny Is Inevitable," May 24, 2010.
D.J. Jaffe	"Involuntary Treatment Saves Lives," *Forbes*, March 7, 2010.
Marney Rich Keenan	"Desperate Veterans Turn to Suicide," *Detroit News*, April 16, 2009.
Peter Korn	"'Suicide Epidemic' Hits Veterans," *Portland Tribune*, August 12, 2008.
Fran Lowry	"Mental Illness Stigma Persists Among Americans," *Medscape*, September 22, 2010. www.medscape.com.
Edie Magnus	"A Deadly Encounter," MSNBC.com, January 20, 2007. www.msnbc.msn.com.
Tara McKelvey	"God, the Army, and PTSD," *Boston Review*, November/December 2009.
Marcia Meier	"Is Criminalizing Mental Health Wise Policy?" *Miller-McCune*, November 18, 2008. www.miller-mccune.com.
IA Robinson and Astrid Rodrigues	"'Mad Pride' Activists Say They're Unique, Not Sick," ABC News, August 24, 2009. http://abcnews.go.com.
Janet Singleton	"Mental Health Parity 2010," *Defenders Online*, November 10, 2009. www.thedefendersonline.com.
Tammy Worth	"Mental Health Parity Act May Affect Your Medical Benefits," *Los Angeles Times*, September 6, 2010.

OPPOSING
VIEWPOINTS®
SERIES

CHAPTER 3

What Mental Health Issues Do Youths Face Today?

Chapter Preface

Native Americans and Alaska Natives between fifteen and twenty-four years old are three times more likely to kill themselves than the general population, for which the suicide rate is about twelve per one hundred thousand. In 2007 the Rosebud Sioux Tribe of South Dakota had a shocking suicide rate of two hundred per one hundred thousand among males between fifteen and twenty-four years old. "We have been sort of identified as the epicenter of suicides in Indian Country," remarks tribal councilman Robert Moore, in an April 2009 article in *U.S. Medicine*. "There is not a single family or tribal citizen at Rosebud that has not been directly impacted by overwhelming suicides in our area." From January to July the following year, sixty-nine children between the ages of one and four visited the Rosebud Comprehensive Health Care Facility for suicidal ideation. "A lot of that is modeling behavior," observes Dan Foster, a clinical psychologist for Indian Health Service in Rosebud, as quoted in a September 2008 article in the *Sicangu Sun Times*. "Some suicides have been very public, hangings in backyards. So many of these little ones we see have witnessed or been affected by it."

The elevated suicide rates of Native American youth are attributed to several factors. For instance, a lack of mental health care services is viewed as a problem. "There is not readily accessible treatment by professionals that is available. It is something that we have to fix," maintains Byron Dorgan, former North Dakota senator and chairman of the Committee on Indian Affairs, quoted in *U.S. Medicine* in April 2009. Moreover, greater prevalences of depression, substance abuse, poverty, and unemployment are found on reservations. At the Menominee Indian Reservation in Wisconsin, where the rate of suicide is thirty per one hundred thousand, half of children live in poor households and unemployment numbers are consistently the worst statewide. To some observers, these issues are the aftereffects of historical oppression on this generation. "They had societies where they had their own norms, their own values, they had customs and traditions . . . all of which kept their life in balance with their community, with their individuality, their families," states Richard Monette, a law professor at the University of Wisconsin. "'They lost all that, and not voluntarily."

The causes of suicide among youth populations are complex and numerous. For teenagers, factors from bullying to mood disorders to antidepressants are speculated to contribute to suicide. In the following chapter, the authors investigate the state of mental health of young Americans.

> *"Suicide is the third ranking cause of death in the 15-to-24 age range."*

Trends in Teen Suicide Are a Serious Problem

Karen Ann Cullota

Karen Ann Cullota is a frequent contributor to the New York Times, Chicago Tribune, *and* O, the Oprah Magazine *and adjunct instructor at Roosevelt University's Department of Communication. In the following viewpoint, Cullota claims that rising suicide rates in the Chicago area—including a cluster of teen suicides since 2007—are a concern for local officials and communities. A 2010 federal study, she adds, shows that young adults between eighteen and twenty-five are at a much higher risk of taking their lives than other age groups. In response, Cullota points out, school districts have responded with programs emphasizing suicide prevention and mental health programs.*

As you read, consider the following questions:

1. According to the author, how does the 2010 suicide rate of Cook County compare to that of previous years?

2. As stated in the viewpoint, what does federal law prohibit regarding school and medical records?

3. How does Richard Kirchhoff describe his late son in the viewpoint?

Just days after his son Ryan's suicide, Richard Kirchhoff decided that his personal heartbreak would not remain a private matter.

"Most people don't like to say the S-word, which is part of the problem," said Kirchhoff, a McHenry County dentist and father of three surviving children who this week [in October 2010] shared the story of his youngest son's 2005 death at age 18.

The presentation, at a McHenry County forum called "Help and Hope," was part of a new suicide prevention and awareness campaign prompted by officials in the McHenry County coroner's office who noticed a spike in suicides in the first nine months of 2010.

The trend is mirrored in DuPage, Kane and Lake counties, where the number of people who have taken their own lives so far this year already is approaching or has overtaken 2009's overall tally.

The statistics also have caught the attention of Chicago-area mental health professionals and school officials. Though observers say they're unsure if this is a short-term phenomenon or hints at the start of a more serious trend, all agree that the rising numbers, provided by each county's coroner or medical examiner, are alarming:

- DuPage County has recorded 78 suicides so far this year, up from 68 suicides in all of 2009.

- Kane County tallied 32 suicides in all of 2009, and 30 so far this year.

- Lake County, where 61 people took their lives last year, has recorded 56 suicides through September.

- McHenry County had 29 suicides in 2009, and has 25 so far in 2010, including the death of Metra Executive Director Phil Pagano, who stepped in front of a commuter train in Crystal Lake in May.

- In Will County, the number of suicides this year stands at 31, compared with 39 all of last year.

- In Cook County, including Chicago, there were about 415 suicides in both 2008 and 2009. Through September of this year, 305 people in Cook County have taken their lives.

Some mental health professionals suggest the recent rise in suicides can be traced in part to the lingering detritus of the economic recession, primarily unemployment, home foreclosures and bankruptcies. Other officials, including Lake County Coroner Richard Keller, said they're also troubled by the recent cluster of teen suicides, including five Barrington High School students who have died since the fall of 2007.

"We obviously have been increasingly concerned about teen suicide," said Jeff Arnett, spokesman for Barrington Community Unit School District 220. "But the fourth student suicide was the tipping point. The entire community and the school district knew that something had to be done."

Arnett said that since 2009, the district has offered an ambitious schedule of suicide prevention and mental health programs, including a forum this month on adolescent depression and bipolar disorder led by professionals with Johns Hopkins Hospital. The district also huddled this week via conference call with officials from Gunn High School in Palo Alto, Calif., an affluent suburb with demographics similar to Barrington's that also has experienced a recent cluster of student suicides.

A 2010 study by the federal Substance Abuse and Mental Health Services Administration found that adults ages 18 to 25 were far more likely to have seriously considered suicide in the last year than those ages 26 to 49, and nearly three times more likely than those 50 or older.

According to the most recent nationwide data from the American Association of Suicidology, 34,598 people in the U.S.—more than 27,000 of them males—took their lives in 2007. Suicide is the third ranking cause of death in the 15-to-24 age range.

Richard McKeon, acting branch chief for suicide prevention at the Substance Abuse and Mental Health Services Administration, said that though some states are reporting a rise in suicide deaths in 2010, it is still too early to determine if the nation's economic malaise is fueling the reported increases.

"We are aware that the economy has had a negative impact on suicide rates, but financial and economic issues are only one factor, and rarely the only factor," McKeon said. "When you're losing your job, your house is in foreclosure and you've just ended a relationship, it can also lead to depression."

Steve Seweryn, an epidemiologist with the Cook County Department of Public Health, agreed that it's often difficult to pinpoint why people take their own lives.

The economy is "basically just an association variable, unless you know that the person who killed themselves lost their job, or it had to do with their economic situation. There may [be] some association with that, but it's hard to say whether that's the reason," he said.

Patrick O'Neil, the coroner in Will County, where suicide rates have been fairly stable in recent years, said financial difficulties and relationship problems tend to be leading causes. Suicides in Will County have also been linked to drug addiction and family history, he said, adding that it's not uncom-

The Insidious National Phenomenon

Despite its higher numbers, suicide tends to make head-lines in national media only when it's a sensational mass suicide by a cult, or when a celebrity or politician takes his or her own life. A teenager's suicide might get a write-up in the hometown paper, but individual reports are usually so locally focused that they miss the insidious national phenomenon: The number of teen victims has been creeping up for years, and these children who are taking pills in their bedrooms or putting loaded guns to their heads are just like other children around the coun-try who are poised to do the same.

Jessica Portner,
One in Thirteen: The Silent Epidemic of Teen Suicide.
Beltsville, MD: Robins Lane Press, 2001.

mon for suicides to occur in the wake of a loved one's death, triggered by a holiday or anniversary.

In response to concerns from mental health professionals across the U.S., McKeon said the Substance Abuse and Mental Health Services Administration recently launched the National Action Alliance for Suicide Prevention. The public health campaign, which aims to help people to recognize the warn-ing signs, also is promoting the national suicide prevention life line, 800-273-TALK, as well as community crisis clinics across the U.S.

"We can't just hope that people who are at risk of suicide will find their way, because the majority of people who die by suicide never found their way to a psychologist or psychiatrist's office," McKeon said. "People need to be able to say the word 'suicide' and not be afraid to ask their loved ones the ques-tion. We may not want to believe that someone we love is thinking about killing themselves, but we need to ask the question and be willing to help."

Five years after his son's suicide, Kirchhoff is a frequent public speaker at area suicide prevention forums, where he often offers advice to families with teenagers. He urges parents of college students, for example, to have them sign a legal release that will give parents access to their children's school and medical records. Federal privacy laws prohibit such records from being disclosed without permission.

Still, he warns parents that many teen suicides are unexpected, including that of his son, whom Kirchhoff described in an essay on the American Foundation for Suicide Prevention's website as a "self-reliant and creative young man," a popular teen with a tightly knit family, many friends and dreams of attending college as a pre-med major.

"From the initial stages of shock and anger, it's been a horrific roller-coaster ride," said Kirchhoff, whose mission is to enlist 10,000 walkers to participate in the annual Out of the Darkness Community Walk—a 20-mile walk along Chicago's lakefront that raises funds for mental health research, suicide prevention programs and survivor support groups. It is a cause that is close to heart, as the Kirchhoff family stepped out together for their first walk shortly after Ryan's death.

"With suicide prevention, we are trying to break down the barriers that go back 1,400 years and that continue to be perpetuated from one generation to the next," Kirchhoff said. "The challenge we face is that unless someone is personally affected by a suicide death, it's not very high on their radar screen." . . .

Freelance reporters Dennis Sullivan, Clifford Ward and Robert Channick contributed to this report.

| *"Talk of a 'surge' in teen suicide, for example, is at best inaccurate."*

Teen Suicide Is Not on the Rise

Jeremy Olson

Jeremy Olson is a reporter for the Star Tribune. *In the following viewpoint, Olson asserts that reports of surges in teen suicide are inaccurate and harmful. Mental health experts in Minnesota warned of a cluster of suicides among students in 2010, but the author counters that the number is on pace for the yearly average. Such views normalize suicide, Olson points out, and the rush among peers to honor victims glamorizes the act. He claims that establishing a connection between suicides is difficult, if not impossible, and prevention programs fail to educate the public on how to honor suicide victims and their families without romanticizing suicide or encouraging depressed teens to seek similar "attention" by committing suicide.*

As you read, consider the following questions:

1. What is the author's opinion on the connection of suicide and bullying?

2. What is the contagion effect, as described by Olson?

3. What example does Olson provide of how social networks glamorize suicide?

Mental-health experts are troubled by a cluster of suicides involving Anoka-Hennepin students this year [2010]—but equally troubled by public reactions and misconceptions that could hamper efforts to prevent more tragedies.

Talk of a "surge" in teen suicide, for example, is at best inaccurate. With 33 teen suicides so far this year, Minnesota is on pace for the average of 42 it has seen annually since 1990.

At worst, that misperception risks "normalizing" suicide, leading teens to accept it as a normal occurrence, said Daniel Reidenberg of the Bloomington-based Suicide Awareness Voices of Education, or SAVE.

"Then when they are confronted or faced with a bad situation," he said, "they think suicide is a normal response."

So much about teen suicide is counterintuitive. The public, the media and politicians tend to seek simple answers to a complex problem. Friends memorialize the dead with bracelets and Facebook pages, which might heal their sorrow but send twisted signals to depressed teens that there is glamour or attention to be gained. Despondent teens perceive suicide as an end to their personal pain, but don't see the torture it brings to those left behind.

It is doubtful that 19-year-old Peter Fredin understood the depth or duration of pain his suicide last November would cause his family.

How his father, Tim Fredin, tried to return to a Prior Lake High School football game last month to regain normalcy—only to circle the parking lot for the first quarter until a police officer stopped him.

Once inside, Fredin leaned against a fence, away from the crowds, watching the Lakers team his son had captained two years earlier. A nearby parent asked if his son was playing.

Fredin, 51, burst into tears.

Placing Blame

In the rush to answer the "why" question—why teens take their own lives—there is often too much emphasis on single factors such as bullying, prevention experts say. While bullying must be addressed, Reidenberg said there is no research to suggest it is any greater a risk factor than divorce, substance abuse, social isolation or other problems.

Mental illness is the most proven risk factor.

"There is no one single thing that leads to suicide, but a lot of people look for an easy answer when suicide happens," said Phyllis Brashler, suicide prevention coordinator for the Minnesota Department of Health. "It's hard. The people left behind really struggle to figure out why this happened."

Some of the focus on bullying has come nationally from the death of Tyler Clementi, the Rutgers University student who killed himself after a sexual encounter with another man was posted online.

Locally, as many as three of the six Anoka-Hennepin suicides in the past year involved teens who were bullied, including Justin Aaberg. His mother has become an advocate for tougher anti-bullying laws and school policies to protect gay students. Two DFL [Democratic-Farmer-Labor Party] lawmakers called for a special legislative session to address the problem.

There are a disproportionate number of gay teens dying by suicide, so advocacy on their behalf is important, Brashler said.

But too much focus on one group can be problematic as well, she said. The Oct. 3 suicide of an Anoka-Hennepin student, she noted, involved someone who wasn't bullied or gay. "I don't want the public to get the sense that it's normal for gay and lesbian youth to attempt suicide," she said.

Not a Benign Myth

Many groups justify their political tactic of "creating a crisis" as necessary to preserving support for the unquestionably fine, underfunded suicide prevention and mental health programs some youths need. But in the end, the myth of a teen suicide epidemic is not benign, no matter how humanely couched. It frightens the public that all young people are lethally out of control. It activates psychiatric industries (which a 1980s congressional investigation found had unconscionably profiteered from spreading fear of teen suicide), programs gearing up to control, moralists eager to censor, police girdling to suppress. We should be pondering why—despite more poverty, overcrowded schools, defunded services, dead-end jobs, family breakup, and incessant denigration by their elders—today's younger generation is *not* descending into self-hatred and suicide.

Russ Kick, ed., Everything You Know Is Wrong: The Disinformation Guide to Secrets and Lies. *New York: The Disinformation Company Ltd., 2002.*

Contagion Effect

Research has long verified the risk of "contagion" for teens, which means one suicide motivates another. Often, it doesn't involve friends, but rather teens with shared circumstances, or depressed teens influenced by media coverage or memorials to teens who died by suicide.

Four Elk River teens died by suicide in 1999–2000. Scott County reported seven teen suicides in 2005—more than in the prior six years combined—including two Prior Lake freshmen who died in one month's time. Two Woodbury High School students died by suicide last spring.

Yet the links in suicide clusters—if they exist—are rarely understood.

The six deaths in Anoka-Hennepin were spread among five schools and had no obvious connections, said Barry Scanlan, a district prevention coordinator.

One challenge is coping with the deaths while not dramatizing them in a way that encourages others.

School administrators often discourage or limit memorials that students place at lockers or in hallways because they send the wrong signals to depressed teens.

Extravagant Memorials Can Cause Unintended Consequences

Social networking has added to that challenge.

Anoka-Hennepin officials intervened earlier this year when a Facebook page to a teen who died by suicide turned troubling, Scanlan said. "Kids were posting statements like, 'You're in a better place, we'll be with you soon.' That's not what we want."

Brashler has mixed feelings about bracelets being sold in memory of Jacob Campbell and Lisa Grijalva, freshmen in the Stillwater schools who died Oct. 12 in an apparent murder-suicide.

While they include a suicide hotline number, they also memorialize the teens by including their names.

"When you think about how that memorial looks to someone who is thinking about suicide," she said, "it takes on a different meaning."

When Dan Krinke died by suicide in March 2005, two weeks after a Prior Lake classmate had taken his own life, his mother tried amid her grief to discourage any more trauma. The family moved the memorial service out of the community, to Richfield, and discouraged students from making T-shirts or school memorials.

Vonnie Krinke wanted to prevent even a slim chance of others experiencing her grief. "It's been long enough that it doesn't screw with my life every day," the mother said this week, "but it's still too hard to talk about."

A community meeting was held after Krinke's death. The Fredins were there.

"I remember thinking, 'Oh, this will never happen to Peter,'" said his mother, Kelli Fredin, because he was an accomplished student, athlete and musician.

Why Peter took his life has bedeviled his parents. Did earlier suicides play a role? Or bad diet at college, or his prior use of an acne medication that some have linked to suicide risks? Or sleep deprivation? That was his unusual topic for a paper he wrote as a University of Minnesota freshman before his death.

Setting aside the "why" question was a first step for Kelli Fredin in her grief. She still finds it hard to leave the house, much less drive near Prior Lake High School. When she visits her daughter in Northfield, the blonds on the St. Olaf campus remind her of her son.

Tim Fredin's tearful encounter at a football game was a step forward. He's been to more games, even approaching Peter's old teachers. Tim and Kelli are blogging to help others grieving over traumatic deaths.

Part of recovery, Tim said, is realizing that he will be grieving for a long time. If teens knew the heartache, would they back away from their rash, fatal judgments?

"They can't," he said, "they just can't imagine the enduring pain."

*"Grim statistics argue strongly for early
detection and intervention and provide
a rationale for mental health screening
among teenagers."*

Mental Health Screenings in Schools Help Children

Richard A. Friedman

Richard A. Friedman is a professor of clinical psychology and director of the psychopharmacology clinic at Weill Cornell Medical College. In the following viewpoint, Friedman recommends mental health screening in schools to uncover depression, anxiety, substance abuse, and trauma among students. The author purports that most youths conceal their emotional issues and give no warning signs to family or friends of attempted suicide. With a likelihood of 20 percent that an adolescent has a treatable psychiatric illness, Friedman maintains, voluntary screening should be routine and universal at schools and reach beyond campuses.

As you read, consider the following questions:

1. What figures does Friedman cite to illustrate the problem of suicide among young people in the United States?

Richard A. Friedman, "Uncovering an Epidemic—Screening for Mental Illness in Teens," *New England Journal of Medicine*, December 28, 2008. Copyright © 2008 *New England Journal of Medicine*. Reproduced by permission.

2. How does the author address the concern that mental health screening invades privacy?

3. What is Friedman's position on the potential for false positives of mental illness through psychiatric evaluation?

Courtney, a 15-year-old from Portland, Oregon, always knew she was different from the other kids. "I had a sense that something was going on, but I was afraid to say anything because I didn't know anyone else had a similar problem," she said. Like thousands of U.S. teens, Courtney participated in a mental health screening program that was offered in her school. "Teenagers have a hard time asking for help," she explained. "Without the screening, I'm not sure how I would have gotten the help I needed."

Before screening, Courtney was part of a silent epidemic of mental illness among teenagers. We know from the National Comorbidity Survey that half of all serious adult psychiatric illnesses—including major depression, anxiety disorders, and substance abuse—start by 14 years of age, and three-fourths of them are present by 25 years of age (see table).[1] Yet the majority of mental illness in young people goes unrecognized and untreated, leaving them vulnerable to emotional, social, and academic impairments during a critical phase of their lives. Even those who receive treatment tend to do so only after a long delay: 6 to 8 years for patients with mood disorders and 9 to 23 years for those with anxiety disorders.

But it is not psychiatric morbidity that makes headlines; rather, it is the most extreme consequence of psychiatric illness: suicide. In the United States, suicide is the third-leading cause of death among persons 15 to 19 years of age. In 2005 alone, according to the Centers for Disease Control and Prevention, 16.9% of U.S. high school students seriously considered suicide, and 8.4% had attempted suicide at least once during the preceding year.

Median Age at the Onset of Mental Disorders

Type of Disorder	Median Age of Onset
Any disorder	14
Anxiety disorder	11
Mood disorder	30
Impulse control disorder	11
Substance-use disorder	20

TAKEN FROM: Richard A. Friedman, "Uncovering an Epidemic—Screening for Mental Illness in Teens," *New England Journal of Medicine*, vol. 355, no. 36, December 28, 2006.

These grim statistics argue strongly for early detection and intervention and provide a rationale for mental health screening among teenagers. The premise is that the primary risk factors for suicide—mood disorder, a previous suicide attempt, and alcohol or substance abuse—can be identified and treated.

Courtney participated in TeenScreen, a large, school-based mental health screening program that was developed under the direction of David Shaffer at Columbia University. The screening is conducted in two stages: teens fill out a short questionnaire and are then interviewed by a master's level social worker or clinical psychologist, who verifies that a positive result is really clinically significant. If it is, the clinician recommends a more comprehensive psychiatric evaluation to the teen and his or her parents. The screening is voluntary and requires the active consent of the parents and assent of the teen. Screening results are confidential and are not shared with school officials or teachers. And since all teenagers who undergo screening also receive a follow-up interview, they cannot be identified by their peers as having screened positive, a system that preserves privacy.

In 2005, the program screened 55,000 young people in 42 states. "About one-third of kids screened positive on the questionnaire, and one-half of those—about 17%—were referred for further evaluation after the clinical interview," said Laurie Flynn, executive director of Columbia University TeenScreen.

There is substantial federal support and funding for such voluntary mental health screening programs. In 2003, the President's New Freedom Commission on Mental Health specifically recommended increased screening for suicidality and mental illness. The commission promoted only programs that were voluntary and conducted with explicit parental consent. In 2004, the Garrett Lee Smith Memorial Act—named for Oregon Senator Gordon Smith's son, who committed suicide when he was 21 years old—earmarked $82 million for youth suicide prevention and early intervention programs.

Not everyone approves of screening teens for psychiatric illness, however. One vocal opponent, Representative Ron Paul (R-TX), who is also a physician, tried unsuccessfully to pass legislation in 2005 banning the use of federal funds for such screening. "I believe the real goal is to make screening mandatory," Paul said. "The motivation might be sincere, but a lot of these folks in government are arrogant and don't believe that parents know what's best for their own kids."

Voluntary screening programs don't interfere with parental rights, but they might well threaten the common—and tragically false—belief that parents are always in a position to know when their child is in trouble and needs help. The fact is that children and teens are notoriously secretive about their own psychopathology: Parents are unaware of 90% of suicide attempts made by teenagers, and the vast majority of teens who attempt suicide give no warning to parents, siblings, or friends.[2] As Courtney put it, "You can be the greatest parent in the world and your kid could still have a serious problem you don't know about."

One 23-year-old woman I interviewed had been screened when she was 15. "I remember being really depressed and suicidal after my cousin sexually molested me," she said. "I couldn't tell my parents about it, and I took an overdose of pills that no one knew about." She says that her meeting with the screening staff helped her to feel comfortable telling her parents what had happened to her and how she felt. "They were shocked and had no idea what I had been going through," she said.

Given the unfortunate stigma that is still attached to mental illness, many observers see screening as an invasion of privacy. Yet suicide has public health implications, for it is, in a sense, contagious: There is ample evidence of suicide clusters among teens, and the relative risk of suicide after exposure to another person's suicide has been estimated to be two to four times as high among teens between the ages of 15 and 19 years as in other age groups.[3]

Some critics worry that asking teens about their mood or suicidal feelings will cause distress or induce suicidal feelings or behavior. In fact, there is evidence to the contrary. In one study, teens were randomly assigned to undergo mental health screening with or without questions that probed suicidal feelings and behavior.[4] The participants who were asked these questions were neither more distressed nor more suicidal than those who were not. In fact, among high-risk students with a known history of depression or suicide attempts, those who had been asked about suicidal thoughts and feelings actually felt less depressed and suicidal after the survey than those who had not been asked such questions.

Some question the effectiveness of mental health screening, arguing that there is little evidence that this intervention prevents young people from committing suicide. Proof that any intervention reduces suicide rates is a high bar to pass, however, since the rarity of suicide would necessitate that a very large population be studied over a long period in order to demonstrate efficacy. Still, preliminary evidence suggests that screening has some positive effects. In one follow-up survey of parents of children who were identified through Teen-Screen as having clinically significant psychiatric symptoms, including suicidal tendencies, 72% reported that their child was doing very well or had significantly improved and was seeing a mental health professional.

Finally, there is concern about the high sensitivity but relatively low specificity of the screening instruments, a combination that leads to many false positive results. The potential consequences of falsely identifying a teen as needing a more thorough psychiatric evaluation seem far less dire, however, than those of failing to identify a suicidal teenager. Stigma is real, but unlike suicide, it doesn't kill.

It is accepted medical practice for teenagers to get frequent physical checkups, even though the odds of finding a serious physical disease in this population are very small. In contrast, the chance that a teen has a treatable psychiatric illness (such as anxiety, mood, or addictive disorder) is nearly 21%.[5] How can we not routinely screen young people for mental illness when it is such an important cause of suffering and death?

I believe that voluntary mental health screening of teens should be universal. But we need to go beyond school-based screening if we are optimally to reach young people who are at risk for psychiatric illness and suicide. Pediatric clinicians are in an ideal position to detect mental illness in young people, and they should be better trained to probe for and recognize the signs and symptoms of major psychiatric disorders.

Courtney put it bluntly: "I'm not sure where I would be today if I didn't get screened. I'm not even sure if I would be here at all."

Notes

1. Kessler RC, Berglund P, Demler O, Jin R, Merikangas KR, Walters EE. Lifetime prevalence and age-of-onset distributions of DSM-IV disorders in the National Comorbidity Survey Replication. Arch Gen Psychiatry 2005;62:593-602. [Erratum, Arch Gen Psychiatry 2005:62:768.]
2. Velez CN, Cohen P. Suicidal behavior and ideation in a community sample of children: maternal and youth reports. J Am Acad Child Adolesc Psychiatry 1988;27:349-56.
3. Gould MS, Wallenstein S, Kleinman M. Time-space clustering of teenage suicide. Am J Epidemiol 1990;131:71-8.
4. Gould MS, Marrocco FA, Kleinman M, et al. Evaluating iatrogenic risk of youth suicide screening programs: a randomized controlled trial. JAMA 2005; 293:1635-43.
5. Shaffer D, Fisher P, Dulcan MK, et al. The NIMH Diagnostic Interview Schedule for Children Version 2.3 (DISC-2.3): description, acceptability, prevalence rates, and performance in the MECA Study. J Am Acad Child Adolesc Psychiatry 1996;35:865-77.

> "*[Mental health screening] undermines basic American freedoms, as parents are coerced to medicate their children, sometimes with severe adverse effects.*"

Mental Health Screenings in Schools Can Harm Children

Nathaniel S. Lehrman

Nathaniel S. Lehrman was the clinical director of Kingsboro Psychiatric Center in Brooklyn, New York, and assistant clinical professor of psychiatry at Albert Einstein College of Medicine and State University of New York Downstate Medical Center. In the following viewpoint, Lehrman insists that mental health screenings in schools harm children and adolescents more than they help them. Designed to identify—and treat primarily with medication—psychiatric illnesses and disorders among students, such screenings often misdiagnose and stigmatize young people as mentally ill, Lehrman asserts. In numerous cases, privacy and parents' rights were infringed, he alleges, and students were forced into treatment and to take unnecessary and harmful psychotropic drugs.

As you read, consider the following questions:

1. Why was Chelsea Rhoades diagnosed with compulsive and social anxiety disorders, according to Lehrman?

2. How does the author link the American Psychiatric Association to higher estimates of the prevalence of mental disorders?

3. How does the screening process produce significant anxiety, in Lehrman's opinion?

According to the president's [George W. Bush's] New Freedom Commission on Mental Health (NFC), all American parents will receive notice from their youngsters' schools of the new screening program during the 2005–2006 school year. It will test for mental illness in the 52 million students and 6 million adults working in schools, and expects to find at least 6 million in need of treatment. The force of government will then urge or compel them to receive that treatment.

But children aren't the only targets. The commission's final report looks forward to having both children and adults screened for mental illnesses during their routine physical examinations.

The sale of psychiatric medications—antipsychotics and antidepressants—rose from $500 million to $20 billion between 1987 and 2004, a 40-fold increase. A pharmaceutical stock analyst recently predicted that continuing to widen our definitions of illness will result in increased sales of medications. This amounts to corporate-sponsored creation of illness, to enhance revenue. With the new screening program, the government-sponsored "discovery" of illness will augment the already existing corporate "promotion of undiscovered illness"—which means even more medication sales. And by allowing experts to define peaceful, law-abiding citizens as ill and in need of treatment (which increasingly is becoming involuntary) the program comes to resemble the witch hunts of 16th-century Europe.

Screening and Its Victims

This is how the program works. In December 2004, as part of the TeenScreen program created to implement the NFC blueprint, Chelsea Rhoades and her Indiana public high school classmates were given a 10-minute, yes-or-no computer test, which had no room for alternate answers or explanations. A few students were not given the test because their parents had opted them out, an option the Rhoades family had not known about in advance.

Shortly after Chelsea took the test, a local mental health center employee told her that she was suffering from obsessive-compulsive disorder because she liked to help clean the house, and from social anxiety disorder because she didn't party much. The worker then suggested that if her condition worsened, her mother should bring her to the center for treatment. Chelsea says all her friends were also told they had something mentally wrong with them. The only youngsters not supposed to be suffering from some mental disorder were those with opt-out slips.

Furious at this intrusion into their privacy and parental rights, the Rhoadeses sounded the alarm. With the help of the Rutherford Institute, they have filed a lawsuit against the school district for failing to inform them about the test or to obtain permission for Chelsea to take it.

Even more frightening was the experience of 13-year-old, black Aliah Gleason, an average, but rather obstreperous seventh-grade student in an Austin, Texas, suburb. After her class was screened for mental illness, her parents were told that she needed further evaluation because she scored high on a suicide rating. She was referred to a university consulting psychiatrist, and thence to an emergency clinic. Six weeks later, a child protection worker appeared at her school, interviewed her, summoned her father to the school, and ordered him to take the girl at once to Austin State (psychiatric) Hospital. When he refused, she took Aliah into emergency custody and had a police officer drive her to the hospital.

During Aliah's five terrible months in hospital, her parents were forbidden to see or speak to her. While there, she was placed in restraints more than 26 times and given at least 12 different psychiatric medications, many of them simultaneously. After that, she spent four more months in a residential facility, where she received even more psychotropic medications.

Despite her caretakers' uncertainty about her clinical diagnosis (and whether she even had a psychiatric illness), her parents had to go to court to have her released. The professionals they chose for her then tapered her off all medication and successfully addressed problems—both hers and the family's. She is now doing well in school, participating in extracurricular activities, and, according to her psychologist, Dr. John Breeding of Austin, recovering her high spirits.

At a Colorado homeless shelter, 50 percent of the 350 young people given the TeenScreen were found to be suicidal risks, and 71 percent screened positive for psychiatric disorders. Although such youngsters are certainly suffering from residential and social instability, and probably from not eating or sleeping properly, the TeenScreen diagnoses lead to medications instead of appropriate interventions.

The particular purpose of children's mental health screening is supposedly to prevent suicide. But the Columbia University TeenScreen program acknowledged that 84 percent of the teens who tested positive were found to be not really at risk. And, as [VH] Sharav points out, an evaluation by the authoritative U.S. Preventive Services Task Force (USPSTF) concluded that screening for suicide failed to demonstrate any benefit at reducing suicide. The report noted that the screening instruments have not been validated. Moreover, there is insufficient evidence that treatment of those identified as high risk reduces either suicide attempts or mortality.

What Is Mental Illness?

What is the mental illness for which we are now screening? Years ago, the term "mental illness" referred only to the insane: people with bizarre ideas who were unable to function socially. Such disabled individuals were social annoyances who might also be dangerous to themselves, others, or both. Other maladaptive psychological patterns such as nervousness or sadness have also been called mental illness, but these produce distress rather than disability. Over the past several decades, however, the term has been expanded to include increasingly more of the thousand natural ills to which the flesh is heir. A recent report from Harvard and the National Institute of Mental Health, for example, says that 46 percent of Americans will at some point in their lives develop a "mental disorder."

Many of those thousand natural ills are included among the 400-odd disorders listed in the latest edition of the American Psychiatric Association's (APA) *Diagnostic and Statistical Manual of Mental Disorders*, the DSM. Calling it the psychiatric bible, Herb Kutchins, professor of social welfare at California State University, Sacramento, and Stuart A. Kirk, professor of social welfare at the University of California at Los Angeles (UCLA), point out that since there are no biological tests, markers, or known causes for most mental illnesses, psychiatric diagnosis is based almost entirely on symptomatology—depression, anxiety, disorganization, obsessive thinking, compulsive behavior, and other subjective symptoms.

Depression, for example, has as many causes as there are people suffering from it: job difficulties, failure to attain expectations, and problems in relationships are but a few. Basing psychiatric diagnosis entirely on symptoms can be compared to making fever a definitive diagnosis; symptoms are not disorders in themselves, but products of other psychological and/or physiological phenomena. The cure of depression—a term rarely used today although a common occurrence yesterday—requires that an individual's particular problems be addressed. Psychiatry's dependence on symptom-based diagnostics is a major reason for the specialty's mounting pessimism.

One reason for higher estimates of the prevalence of mental disorders is that the APA keeps adding new disorders and more behaviors to the manual, as Kutchins and Kirk point out. The increase in the number of these disorders, along with the greatly increased use of new medications to treat them, parallels the increase in individuals disabled by these disorders. Rates for psychiatric disability in America have risen from 3.38 per thousand in 1954; to 13.75 in 1987, when the atypical antipsychotics and SSRI antidepressants were introduced; to 19.69 in 2003. The number of patient care episodes—the amount of care given, as measured by the number of people treated each year for mental illness at psychiatric hospitals, residential facilities for the mentally ill, and ambulatory care facilities—rose similarly: from 1,028 per 100,000 population in 1955; to 3,295 in 1987; and to 3,806 in 2000. Since the start of the "medication era," the number of mentally disabled people has risen nearly sixfold.

How the History of ADHD Predicts the Effects of Screening

Kutchins and Kirk point out that children are considered to exhibit signs of attention deficit hyperactivity disorder (ADHD) when they are deceitful, break rules, can't sit still or wait in lines, have trouble with math, don't pay attention to details, don't listen, don't like to do homework, lose their school assignments or pencils, or speak out of turn. This common childhood behavior is defined as a disorder by the psychiatry department of the New York University (NYU) School of Medicine. ADHD is now diagnosed in 6 to 9 percent of school-age children and 4 percent of adults. Its "symptoms"—acting impulsively; easy distractibility; interrupting others; constant fidgeting or moving; and difficulty in paying attention, waiting one's turn, planning ahead, following instructions, or meeting deadlines—can be found in any of us. With diagnosis and treatment, the department contends, ADHD symptoms can be substantially decreased.

The process through which ADHD became accepted is important, but little recognized. In 1980, the list of symptoms then called ADD (attention deficit disorder) was first accepted into the DSM. Seven years later, hyperactivity was added, thus making ADHD. Within a year, 500,000 youngsters were assigned this diagnosis.

A few years later, ADHD was classified as a disability, and a cash incentive program was initiated for low-income families with children diagnosed with ADHD. A family could get $450 a month for each child so labeled, and the cost of treatment and medication for low-income children would be covered by Medicaid. Then in 1991, schools began receiving educational grants of $400 annually for each ADHD child. The same year, the U.S. Department of Education classified the disorder as a handicap, which required special services to be provided to each disabled child.

By 1996, close to $15 billion was spent annually on the diagnosis, treatment, and study of this supposed neuropsychiatric disorder. Recently, public health officials in the United States, Canada, and the United Kingdom have issued warnings about previously known but undisclosed risks associated with the stimulant medications used to treat ADHD.

What has happened with ADHD presages what can be expected from government-sponsored mental health screening. One example is the case of the first-grade son of Patricia Weathers. After a school psychologist diagnosed the "disorder," she was pressured into medicating him.

"The medication eventually made him psychotic," she said. But when she stopped giving it to him, the school reported her to state child protection officials for "child abuse." Weathers cofounded AbleChild (www.AbleChild.org) and filed a lawsuit against school officials.

"We have 1,000 stories like this," she states. Meanwhile, her son is now 15 and "doing fine."

Rep. Ron Paul, M.D., (R-TX) a congressman who has been a physician for more than 30 years, has criticized government agencies for charging parents with child abuse if they refuse to drug their children. Some parents have even had their children taken from them for refusing to give them medications.

Mrs. Weathers's experience is far from unique. According to Dr. Andrew Mosholder of the FDA's [Food and Drug Administration] Office of Drug Safety, about 2.5 million children in this country between ages 4 and 17 currently take ADHD drugs, 9.3 percent of 12-year-old boys, and 3.7 percent of 11-year-old girls. And although these medications have been used for years, the harm they can cause to the heart and circulatory system, and the psychiatric difficulties they can produce, are only now being publicly discussed.

No matter how we define mental illness in children or adults, it cannot be diagnosed by simple screening. Nobody can, by merely looking at someone else, or even on the basis of a questionnaire, differentiate the transient emotional disturbances we all have from those that last longer.

The ephemeral nature of suicidal ideation and depressive feelings among teens is specifically mentioned by the Columbia TeenScreen report. Screenings won't prevent suicide because those who are contemplating it usually won't tell. Indeed, the screening process itself can produce significant anxiety among those in whom mental illness is being "diagnosed." Such efforts to find their troubles by frightening people, and thus aggravating those troubles, are misdirected.

Only when gross insanity exists can mental illness be recognized on inspection, and then we need neither experts nor screening.

Troubled people can indeed benefit from good mental health care. But good treatment requires that a physician actually examine a patient and address that individual's unique problems, with the patient's knowledge and consent. This requires time, and busy practitioners are often under severe time constraints. Thus they are pressured to quickly prescribe medications to relieve symptoms that are often transient even if untreated.

In my opinion, relying on medication as the definitive treatment of psychiatric complaints, rather than addressing their real causes in patients' lives, is responsible for the gross overuse of psychiatric medications, especially among children, but also among seniors:

- Twenty-nine million prescriptions were written last year [2005–2006] in the United States for Ritalin and similar medications to treat ADHD, 23 million of them for children.

- From 60 to 70 percent of children in foster care in Massachusetts are now being given psychiatric medications.

- About 40 to 50 percent of students arrive at some colleges with psychiatric prescriptions.

- Approximately 41 percent of prescriptions for one group of 765,000 people over 65 were for psychotropics.

- As many as 75 percent of elderly, long-term-care nursing home residents in another study were being given psychotropics.

The screening program will aggravate this already unfortunate situation.

No Medical or Societal Purpose

Good intentions notwithstanding, the mental health screening program created by the president's NFC probably will harm thousands of Americans by giving them stigmatizing diagnoses that can follow them for the rest of their lives. The program's government-sponsored promotion of long-term medications will compound the harm, as the experience with ADHD has shown.

As Sharav points out, screening for mental illness serves no medical or societal purpose. Screening will, however, do much to increase the benefits to the drug manufacturers and to the mental health provider industry. Good psychiatric care is voluntary, and based on trust between patient and physician. The involuntary government-sponsored mental health screening program, as demonstrated by the cases of Aliah Gleason and Chelsea Rhoades, represents psychiatric malpractice.

Their cases also demonstrate how the program undermines basic American freedoms, as parents are coerced to medicate their children, sometimes with severe adverse effects.

We need to start to undo psychiatry's 50 years of overdependence on psychopharmacology, rather than expanding it through mental health screening.

Periodical and Internet Sources Bibliography

The following articles have been selected to supplement the diverse views presented in this chapter.

Rick Bayer	"Mental Illness & Suicide in Teens: Myths, Facts and Solutions," *Alternatives*, Spring 2007.
Brendan Borrell	"Pros and Cons of Screening Teens for Depression," *Los Angeles Times*, August 3, 2009.
Charles Q. Choi	"National Screening for Mental Illness in Teens Inspires Controversy," *Scientific American*, January 23, 2007.
Barbara Cotter	"Height, Weight, and Mental Health: Checkups for Teens to Evaluate Mind and Body," *Gazette*, May 7, 2010.
Cian Denihan	"Antidepressants Prevent Suicides in Young People," *Irish Medical Times*, July 29, 2010.
C. Munsey	"Antidepressants and Children: Too Little or Too Much?" *Monitor on Psychology*, November 2009.
Grace Rubenstein	"Suicide Prevention Can Start in School," Edutopia, November 10, 2009. www.edutopia.org.
Christina A. Samuels	"Schools' Role in Mental-Health Care Uneven, Experts Say," *Education Week*, May 1, 2007.
Andy Sedlak	"Teen Suicides on the Rise," *Middletown Journal* (Middletown, OH), December 6, 2010.
Kim Wein	"Drug Me, Please," *Good Times* (Santa Cruz, CA), December 28, 2009.
Robert F. Wilson, Mei Tang, Kelly Schiller, and Kerry Sebera	"No Child Overlooked: Mental Health Triage in the Schools," *Michigan Journal of Counseling*, March 22, 2009.

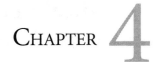

CHAPTER 4

What Treatments for Mental Illness Are Effective?

Chapter Preface

Deep brain stimulation is a surgical procedure being researched as a way to treat depression. Controlled by a pacemaker implanted in the chest, several electrodes—each a millimeter wide—are placed in regions of the brain that influence mood, emitting electrical pulses that affect neural activity. Developed in 1987 by French researchers for the treatment of movement disorders, deep brain stimulation has been approved by the US Food and Drug Administration for treating Parkinson's disease, dystonia, and tremor, as well as for severe cases of obsessive-compulsive disorder.

Diane Hire, a participant in a clinical trial for deep brain stimulation, suffered from debilitating depression for decades; she stopped leaving her house and attempted suicide several times. "It was a really black, dismal existence," Hire revealed in a September 13, 2007, article in *Popular Science*. Medication and treatment, including more than seventy rounds of electroconvulsive therapy, did not improve her condition. But immediately after the surgery in 2007, the implant working, she smiled for the first time in years and said, "I feel like I could get up and do all sorts of things." Hire eventually recovered from depression, losing the 120 pounds she gained while depressed. "I wake up every day happy to be alive. I wake up looking forward to what is ahead. I am who I was," she stated at a conference in 2008 (as quoted in an article by Jamie Talan on dana.org). "I am not a new person or a changed person. I am who I was."

The procedure, however, is still in the experimental stage. "We want to treat depression like we treat heart disease," explains Helen Mayberg, a neurologist who led pioneering research of the treatment, also quoted in the article by Talan. "If something goes wrong, it's over. We are being very careful." Patients face several risks from the surgery such as brain hemorrhage, stroke, and infection. Side effects range from seizures to hallucinations to brain damage.

Deep brain stimulation is one of the most novel approaches to the rehabilitation of depression. Other recent developments include the return of electroconvulsive therapy and the management of schizophrenia without medication. In the following chapter, the authors explore various treatments for mental illness.

> *"Most people might be quicker to associate electroshock therapy with torture rather than healing. But since the 1980s, the practice has been quietly making a comeback."*

Electroconvulsive Therapy Can Be Helpful

Melissa Dahl

Melissa Dahl is a health writer and editor at MSNBC.com. In the following viewpoint, Dahl writes that electroconvulsive therapy (ECT) is gaining traction as an effective, fast-acting treatment for severe depression. She proposes that many psychiatrists consider ECT the most successful way to treat patients who do not respond to antidepressants and imperative for preventing suicide attempts. ECT recipients, Dahl adds, report a marked elevation in mood after several sessions of the treatment. Critics cite cognitive side effects and possible brain damage, but understanding how ECT works would be a boon to psychiatry, the author maintains.

As you read, consider the following questions:

1. How is modern ECT performed?

2. How does the author characterize memory loss as the result of ECT in most cases?

3. How did ECT impact Bill Russell's life after seven months, according to Dahl?

When Bill Russell tells people that his severe depression was relieved by shock therapy, the most common response he gets is: "They're *still* doing that?"

Most people might be quicker to associate electroshock therapy with torture rather than healing. But since the 1980s, the practice has been quietly making a comeback. The number of patients undergoing electroconvulsive therapy, as it's formally called, has tripled to 100,000 a year, according to the National Mental Health Association [currently known as Mental Health America].

During an ECT treatment, doctors jolt the unconscious patient's brain with an electrical charge, which triggers a grand mal seizure. It's considered by many psychiatrists to be the most effective way to treat depression especially in patients who haven't responded to antidepressants. One 2006 study at Wake Forest School of Medicine in North Carolina found that ECT improved the quality of life for nearly 80 percent of patients.

"It's the definitive treatment for depression," says Dr. Kenneth Melman, a psychiatrist at Swedish Medical Center in Seattle who practices ECT. "There aren't any other treatments for depression that have been found to be superior to ECT."

In fact, antidepressants—the most widely used method for treating depression—don't work at all for 30 percent of patients.

But some doctors and past patients say that the risks of shock therapy, such as memory loss, are too high a price to pay for the temporary benefits.

Despite convulsive therapy's 70-year history, doctors still aren't sure exactly how ECT works to ease depression. What they do know is that ECT works very quickly, with many patients reporting their depression lifting after just a few sessions—and in patients with severe depression, a fast-acting treatment is considered imperative to prevent a suicide attempt.

Russell, who lives in Mill Creek, Wash., has struggled with depression and obsessive-compulsive disorder since he was in high school. But his depression began to weigh on him like a lead coat in the spring of 2007, after the pace at his job as an electronics technician quickened, and he couldn't keep up and became overwhelmed. Every night that spring, he came home from work and went straight to bed. He was barely eating and dropped 40 pounds in three months. At his lowest point, he formed a plan to kill himself.

As his depression worsened, he was hospitalized, and at one point was on eight different antidepressants and antianxiety drugs, but none of them helped. It wasn't until he tried ECT as a desperate last resort that he was helped. His depression started to lift after the first week of treatments.

A Crucial Treatment—or Brain Damage?

But not everyone responds as well as Russell, say critics of the treatment who warn that the cognitive side effects, such as memory loss, are too severe, and that the fuzzy, foggy state of mind that ECT initially causes simply makes patients temporarily forget about their sadness. (Nearly every ECT patient experiences confusion, inability to concentrate and short-term memory loss during the treatment.)

"We talk about cognitive deficits and memory loss—really, that's brain damage," says John Breeding, a psychologist in private practice in Austin, Texas. Breeding has counseled several past ECT patients, who say they've suffered long-term cognitive damage as a result of electroshock. He's working to ban ECT in his state, and he runs the website EndofShock .com.

Breeding and other skeptics argue that ECT is nothing more than a quick fix: Once the treatments stop, the depression returns. And at least one study backs that claim: In 2001, Columbia University researchers found that without follow-up medications, depression returned in 84 percent of ECT patients within six months.

Most patients are given three treatments a week for a total of six to 12 sessions. After that, once the patient's mood has reached a plateau, the psychiatrist may stop the ECT sessions and prescribe an antidepressant. If someone hasn't responded well to antidepressants in the past, ECT won't do anything to change that. For those patients, a doctor may prescribe a different antidepressant from those that had failed before. Or those patients may need once-a-month follow-up treatments, called maintenance ECT, which can continue for years.

The American Psychiatric Association [APA] approves ECT as a "safe and effective" treatment for depression and other mental illnesses, such as schizophrenia and catatonia. Under the APA's guidelines, an anesthesiologist, a psychiatrist and a recovery nurse must be present during a treatment, and the treatment must be voluntary, unless the patient is unable to provide informed consent. It's not recommended for the very old, children or those with heart conditions. Insurance covers treatments for most patients.

Despite the APA's approval, for the general public, shock therapy still conjures images from *One Flew Over the Cuckoo's Nest*;—it's Jack Nicholson being electrocuted, making terrible grimaces as his body convulses.

"Quite frankly, the stigma pushes people away from it, and it pushes some psychiatrists away from even recommending

ECT," says Dr. William McDonald, an Emory University psychiatrist who reviews the APA's guidelines on electroconvulsive and electromagnetic therapies. "But most of the stigma related to ECT really is related to misconception."

Psychiatrists readily admit that in the early days, ECT absolutely was a cruel procedure. And because the treatment has lingered in the shadows of psychiatry for decades, many people still associate it with its sketchy past.

Convulsive therapy was introduced in the mid-1930s, when scientists discovered that by triggering a seizure, they were able to shock psychiatric patients back into a functioning state of mind. It was designed to be a treatment for curing schizophrenia, but doctors found it also seemed to benefit patients with depression, bipolar disorder and catatonia.

Convulsions Strong Enough to Break Bones

During the '40s and '50s, it was one of the only available methods for treating mental illness, so it was often overused. Even when doctors adhered to the standards of the day, it was a harrowing procedure: As patients were shocked with electricity, they were wide awake, feeling their bodies' convulsions, which were sometimes severe enough to break bones.

At its peak of popularity during the early 1960s, about 300,000 U.S. patients a year received shock therapy.

Treatments both then and now require about the same amount of electricity—somewhere between 3 and 100 joules depending on the patient. (For context, one joule is the amount of energy it takes to lift an apple three feet in the air; 100 joules is enough energy to power a desktop computer.) But in a modern ECT treatment, patients are under anesthesia during the entire process, asleep and unaware of the electrical currents charging through their brains. A muscle relaxant prevents their bodies from jerking around once the seizure is triggered; in fact, the patient hardly moves at all.

Other Indications for ECT

Small studies have found ECT [electroconvulsive therapy] effective in the treatment of catatonia, a symptom associated with mood disorders, schizophrenia, and medical and neurological disorders. ECT is also reportedly useful in treating episodic psychoses, atypical psychoses, obsessive-compulsive disorders, and delirium and such medical conditions as neuroleptic malignant syndrome, hypopituitarism, intractable seizure disorder, and the on-off phenomenon of Parkinson's disease. ECT may also be the treatment of choice for depressed suicidal pregnant women who require treatment and cannot take medication; for geriatric and medically ill patients who cannot take antidepressant drugs safely; and perhaps even for severely depressed and suicidal children and adolescents who may be less likely to respond to antidepressant drugs than are adults. ECT is not effective in somatization disorder (unless accompanied by depression), personality disorders, and anxiety disorders.

Benjamin J. Sadock and Virginia A. Sadock,
Kaplan & Sadock's Concise Textbook of Clinical Psychiatry.
Baltimore, MD: Lippincott Williams & Wilkins, 2008.

When Russell, 43, initially was considering ECT, he and his wife, Sue, did extensive research and had lengthy conversations with his doctor about the realities of the treatment. While he was desperate to find a way out of his depression, he was still terrified of shock therapy. "At first, I thought of Frankenstein," Bill Russell says. "I thought, 'That's drastic, that causes brain damage—there's no way I want to do that.'"

After weighing the risks with the depression he just couldn't shake, he made an appointment with Melman, the doctor at Seattle's Swedish Medical Center.

The hospital is being renovated, which has shunted the ECT suite to a somewhat unfortunate location: the basement, just down the hall from the emergency room.

"I can remember seeing one person (in the waiting room) that really looked out of it, just like a zombie, sort of," Bill Russell says. "I was just thinking, 'Oh God, no, I don't want to end up like that.'

"We almost got up and felt like saying, 'No way, forget it,'" he remembers.

A quick husband-wife huddle reminded them that they were now down to their last idea for relieving Bill's depression, because psychotherapy, medications and hospitalization hadn't helped. They resolved to give shock therapy a shot.

An anesthesiologist put Russell to sleep as he lay flat on a gurney. After he was out, nurses gave him a muscle relaxant through an IV, paralyzing his body. They placed a blood pressure cuff on his lower right calf, preventing the muscle relaxant from flowing to his right foot, which they would rely on during the treatment to twitch and tell them when a seizure was happening.

Melman placed one handheld electrode at the crown of Russell's head, and the other at his right temple, sending electrical currents through his brain for about two seconds while Russell lay perfectly still—only his right foot slightly moving.

During his first month of treatments, Russell's world was like a foggy, fuzzy dream. He was in the thick of ECT's most common side effect: short-term memory loss. Before his wife left for work each day, she papered their home in Post-its— Remember to take your pills! Here's my phone number!—and took his keys and license, because if he hopped in the car, he might not remember how to find his way back.

"It was like living with Ozzy Osbourne," Sue Russell remembers. Between July and December 2007, Bill Russell had 20 ECT treatments. He went back to work part-time after the first three months of ECT.

The severity of memory loss varies from patient to patient, and in most cases it's limited to the weeks before and after. While Russell had a somewhat innocuous experience, Melman recalls a former patient whose relative died during the weeks of her ECT treatments. Her family had to tell her again and again of their loss.

Adverse Effects Devastate Patients

Some former electroshock patients say that the treatment's side effects don't end with short-term memory loss. Juli Lawrence, who had 12 ECT treatments in 1994, says it caused long-term cognitive damage. She says she now has trouble learning new things, and she still has problems with her memory.

"My family and I were told it would cure the depression and it did not," says Lawrence, who's 46 and lives in Long Island, N.Y. "After holding out all this hope that it would be the final answer, it didn't happen. I was completely devastated. On top of that, I had memory loss, and on top of that, I had cognitive damage."

Lawrence runs a website called Ect.org, which has a message board filled with hundreds of former ECT patients who call themselves "electroshock survivors." They say they've suffered brain damage as a result of ECT. But as no studies have established a link between ECT and long-term cognitive damage, evidence of long-term harm remains anecdotal.

But for most patients, ECT does provide near-immediate relief, say many psychiatrists. It tends to work best in people who've had a hard, fast fall into depression—people like Karen, a current patient at Melman's. (Because Karen is still going through treatments, she requested that her last name not be used.) Just one month after her first treatment in June, Karen, who is in her early 30s, returned to work part-time.

There were a few awkward exchanges in her first week back, Karen says, when she realized she had forgotten the names of certain co-workers. Her job as a communications liaison for a nonprofit in Seattle involves a lot of international travel, and after returning to work she had trouble recalling the details of some trips. ECT even erased an entire country from her memory—there are pictures of Karen on a trip to Ethiopia that she can't remember at all.

After 12 treatments, she says she's 90 percent better. "There's a little bit of gnawing anxiety . . . what if this happens again?"

Because ECT has a high relapse rate for depression, doctors prescribe psychotherapy or medications after the final ECT session. For skeptics of ECT like Breeding, the Texas psychologist, that proves that ECT is just a quick fix, and it doesn't work to relieve depression in the long run.

"Sometimes you need a quick fix," says Dr. Alan Gelenberg, a clinical professor of psychiatry at the University of Wisconsin-Madison. He points out that depression itself has a high relapse rate. And a 2001 Oxford University study found that depression returned in about 40 percent of patients who stopped taking an antidepressant. "But you do need to attend to long-term issues in any way you can: medications, talk therapy or periodic readministrations of ECT."

Researchers like Dr. Sarah Lisanby, professor of clinical psychiatry at Columbia University, are working to find new, less traumatic therapies that rival ECT's efficacy for relieving depression.

Solving the Mystery

But part of Lisanby's research is also devoted to uncovering how ECT works.

"Solving the mystery of how ECT works is going to be important for advancements in the field of psychiatry, because ECT has unparalleled efficacy," Lisanby says. "Understanding why ECT is so much more effective than medications could help the field develop more effective treatments—and safer treatments."

Because so much of ECT is still not understood, and because of its stigma, some psychiatrists treat ECT as a dire last resort. Instead of being considered a last option, Melman and other proponents of ECT wish that it was considered a next option.

"It can be considered much earlier than it is for most patients today," Melman says. "Patients suffer with depression either with no response or partial response (to antidepressants), and for years they limp along with terrible depression."

For Bill Russell, seven months have passed since his last ECT treatment. He's now taking antidepressants, and he's had some bad days that brought him close to scheduling a booster ECT treatment. But both Russells say that their life is essentially back to the way it's always been in their 12 years of marriage. And they both insist that without ECT, Bill wouldn't be here.

"It was like a kick-start, like starting over," Bill Russell says. "When I was done with the treatments and the fog started to clear, it was like waking up from a bad dream."

> *"Today, between 100,000 and 200,000 Americans undergo [electroconvulsive therapy] each year. But not everyone is convinced that's a good thing."*

Electroconvulsive Therapy May Not Be Helpful

Matt Snyders

Matt Snyders is a writer based in Minneapolis-St. Paul, Minnesota. In the following viewpoint, the author maintains that electroconvulsive therapy (ECT) for severe depression and other psychiatric disorders may be ineffective and harmful. According to Snyders, some psychologists warn that ECT causes brain damage, resulting in memory loss commonly seen in recipients, and has a near 100 percent relapse rate. Nonetheless, he states that mental health courts frequently order ECT for ill individuals deemed incompetent by virtue of being committed, such as a Minnesota man who was forced into shock treatment on an outpatient basis.

As you read, consider the following questions:

1. What happened to Ray Sandford during ECT, in the author's words?

2. How does Snyder describe Sandford's predicament in
   court on June 10, 2008?

3. How did MindFreedom International stop Sandford
   from undergoing ECT, according to Snyders?

R ay Sandford doesn't want to do this.

On a sunny yet cool mid-April morning, the pear-shaped
54-year-old emerges from the front door of his ranch-style
group home in Columbia Heights. Wearing a black wind-
breaker and gray sweatpants, he grips the handle of his four-
pronged cane and plods begrudgingly toward the street. One
of Sandford's caretakers, a large woman wearing all purple,
follows perfunctorily behind to see him to his destination.

He's told them repeatedly he doesn't want to do this.

He ambles forward. There's nothing he can do now. No
sense in fighting it. Not now.

A 20-passenger Anoka transit bus idles along the curb
awaiting his arrival. A short, swarthy driver assists Sandford.
The bus slowly pulls away and embarks on the 12-mile ride to
Mercy Medical Center in Coon Rapids.

Upon arrival, Sandford walks through the automatic sliding doors and assumes his position in a wheelchair. He's
whisked to a room on the fifth floor where nurses poke an IV
through his fleshy forearm. He's given a muscle relaxant and
general anesthesia. Within 30 seconds, the room dissolves.
He's out cold.

Assistants lay him out on his back. A doctor places electrodes on either side of Sandford's cranium. Cords extend
from the electrodes, connecting to what appears to be an anti-
quated stereo set. A couple of dials protrude from the
machine's display. A physician flips an unassuming switch.

A three-second burst of 140 volts blasts through Sandford's
brain. While he's totally unconscious, Sandford's torso jerks
up and down. His arms and legs writhe only slightly, steadied

by muscle relaxants coursing through his veins. Sandford's toes curl downward, as if his feet were trying to ball up into fists. He's experiencing a grand mal seizure.

Two minutes later, it's over. Sandford will feel a bit woozy the rest of the day, but there'll be no lasting pain. His short-term memory is the only thing that will suffer.

But he'll still remember quite clearly that he never wanted to do this.

"They can literally tie me up, put me in ambulance, and bring me in to get shock treatments," he says. "I don't fight it, because there's nothing I can do by that time. You want to know how I feel? I don't like it at all."

A Controversial Medical Procedure

Introduced to America in 1939, electroconvulsive therapy is one of the most controversial medical procedures still in practice. Not much is known about how or why it works. Even so, by the end of World War II, every reputable hospital in the world performed the procedure.

"It was a very useful treatment because there was no treatment like it before," says ECT proponent Dr. Max Fink, widely regarded as the grandfather of American ECT and a professor of psychiatry at Stony Brook University in New York. "At the time, every state was troubled by the fact that they were building bigger and bigger hospitals for the mentally ill. Once ECT caught on, the number of hospital beds for mental illness was reduced sharply."

After the advent of psychotropic drugs in the 1950s, however, ECT appeared to be going the way of the lobotomy. Prescription meds were suddenly viewed as a more reliable and humane alternative.

But by the early '80s, something unexpected happened: antidepressants and other psychotropics turned out not to be the panacea everyone hoped they would be.

"Many doctors had patients who had been given the best care in the major centers of the world with pills, but they still had patients who were very, very sick," says Dr. Fink. "So they turned to doctors who were using ECT devices, and one by one, hospital by hospital, ECT was reintroduced. Most of the reintroduction occurred at the end of the 1980s and beginning of the 1990s. By now, there aren't many psychiatric hospitals that don't have ECT."

Today, between 100,000 and 200,000 Americans undergo the procedure each year. But not everyone is convinced that's a good thing.

"When you induce a grand mal convulsion by sending 100-plus volts of electricity in the brain, you're going to create damage," says Dr. John Breeding, an Austin, Texas-based psychologist and self-described ECT abolitionist. "This is most easily seen with memory loss that many patients experience. You're talking major voltage directly into the temporal lobes of the brain. And the data is very clear that there's close to a 100 percent relapse rate, which means patients have to keep coming back and suffer further brain damage. This is referred to as 'maintenance ECT,' rather than as a failed treatment, which is what it really is."

Even more controversial is the practice of forced, court-ordered electroconvulsive treatment. Neither the American Psychiatric Association nor activist groups have estimates on how many Americans undergo forced ECT annually, but there were 41 cases in Hennepin County last year [in 2008].

Ray Sandford was one of them. But unlike the others, he's not going quietly, opting instead to take his fight to the public arena. A small army of mental-health activists has now taken up a national-scale PR [public relations] campaign on his behalf, painting him as something of a real-life R.P. McMurphy from *One Flew Over the Cuckoo's Nest*.

"This case is particularly egregious," says Dr. Breeding. "Ray Sandford was really the first I heard of somebody being shocked on an outpatient basis."

A Grim Prognosis

Marilyn Sandford had particularly high hopes for her eldest son. When her three boys, along with their neighborhood friends, would play in a vast sandpit on the far side of their two-acre estate in Eagan, it was clear, even from a distance, that Raymond was in charge.

"He was exceptionally bright and had a real gift for verbal persuasion," says Marilyn. "Those boys were a pack, and he was the leader of the pack. We assumed he'd make an excellent salesman."

Ray's father, a contractor by trade, built the family's blue two-story home himself, outfitting the stately split-level with a cathedral ceiling and spiral staircase. With no mortgage to pay and the postwar housing boom providing lucrative work for her husband, Marilyn was able to quit her job as a polio nurse and devote her time to raising the boys.

As Ray entered adolescence, he grew enamored of real estate, memorizing local lot prices and market fluctuations. His goal, he told his parents matter-of-factly, was to be a millionaire by the age of 21.

Shortly after Ray's 17th birthday, it became clear that something was wrong with him. Ray, who had always gotten exceptional grades at Sibley High in Mendota Heights, suddenly dropped out his senior year. He emptied his college fund—about $3,000 his parents had saved up—and bought his own lot in a trailer park in Lilydale, eight miles north.

At first, Marilyn chalked up her son's bizarre behavior to adolescent angst.

"It's very hard to come to terms with the fact that your eldest and very promising child is mentally ill," she says. "That's not something you're ever ready for."

But as Ray's recklessness continued to escalate, Marilyn was forced to confront reality. Out to run some errands, Marilyn glanced in her rearview mirror to see Ray following close behind in his '63 Impala—too close. He whizzed past her, then abruptly stopped. He peeled out around her, nearly smashing into oncoming traffic, then stopped again.

Ray's thoughts and speech, meanwhile, grew more and more disjointed. When Ray was 19, Marilyn's father, a country doctor, visited the family. After supper, he took Marilyn aside and told her what she already knew: "You need to get that boy checked out."

She brought her son to Hastings Mental Hospital. After observing Ray and hearing Marilyn's account of his behavior, the doctors gave Marilyn a grim prognosis: "Your son suffers from severe manic depression. We recommend he be institutionalized."

Ray's new home would be Hastings Mental Hospital, an austere brick building.

"Now his brother is a doctor, his sister is a doctor, another brother is a successful engineer, and then another brother owns and manages property," Marilyn says ruefully. "They're all doing very well and here he is, the leader—and each hospitalization leaves him a little less well-off financially. So now he really has nothing."

In 2005, Marilyn, then 76 and eyeing her own mortality, contacted Lutheran Social Services, the state's largest nonprofit provider of health care, and asked them to act as legal guardian and caretaker for Ray. She would no longer have any legal say in his future. For Marilyn, it was a difficult but necessary decision.

"I have high blood pressure; I could die tomorrow," she says. "It's ridiculous to assume I could be responsible for someone else's life at this point. I knew we needed to find him a conservator."

By 2006, Ray Sandford had transferred to Community Behavioral Health Hospital in Willmar. Shortly after the move, his manic spells worsened. Sandford grew frustrated with the confines, which only exacerbated his psychosis. According to a report later submitted to a mental court, Sandford was "grossly psychotic, yelling violently and smearing feces all over, urinating wherever and whenever he felt like it."

The meds weren't working. The time had come for an alternative.

In January 2008, staff at Willmar approached Dr. Kevin Turnquist, a psychiatrist who specializes in schizophrenia. Four months after meeting Ray, the doctor petitioned to impose electroconvulsive therapy on the 54-year-old.

At the May 13 hearing in the basement of St. Paul's Regions Hospital, Ramsey County District Judge Teresa R. Warner heard from Dr. Turnquist, as well as from two court-appointed medical examiners who testified that Ray was "not in a position to weigh the benefits versus the risks of ECT treatment."

The hearing was quick, lasting barely a half hour.

"The Court considered the respondent's family and community, as well as his moral, religious, and social values," ruled Judge Warner. "Based on these considerations, a reasonable person would authorize treatment with electroconvulsive therapy."

The Ritual

The ritual always begins the same.

Just after 6 p.m. Sandford hears a knock at the door. It's his caretakers. They've come to raid his refrigerator.

"No more food for the rest of the night, Ray. Doctor's orders."

After purging the fridge of sandwich meat and the shelves of Doritos, they march upstairs and stash the provisions in a padlocked compartment.

Striking to the Core

Defenders of ECT [electroconvulsive therapy] say that because of the addition of anesthesia to make the procedure painless, the horribleness of ECT is entirely a thing of the past. This argument misses the point. It is the mental disorientation, the memory loss, the lost mental ability, the realization after awaking from the "therapy" that the essence of one's very *self* is being destroyed by the "treatment" that induces the terror—not only or even primarily physical suffering. ECT, or electroshock, strikes to the core personality and is terrifying for this reason.

Lawrence Stevens,
"Psychiatry's Electroconvulsive Shock Treatment:
A Crime Against Humanity," Antipsychiatry Coalition, 2010.
www.antipsychiatry.org.

It's not a cruel trick; if Sandford ever succumbed to a midnight hankering for a bologna sandwich, it might very well prove to be his last. That's because, should any food still be sloshing around his stomach during next morning's ECT-induced seizure, there's a good chance he'd vomit and choke to death on the table.

Which is why he doesn't utter a word of protest as they carry his groceries away, or when his stomach starts growling at 10 p.m.

"There's nothing fun about it," he says of the fasting, and leaves it at that.

Of greater concern to him is the procedure itself. He knows he'll be unconscious during the ordeal, that it will be painless. Still, he's a bit anxious.

"You don't know if you're going to wake up," he says, his eyes widening as he confronts his own mortality. "It's not very likely, but it's still *possible*. When I did the first couple of them, I was a lot more scared than I am now."

He did those first few willingly—anything to get out of the hospital, which he found to be oppressive. It seemed like a fair trade-off.

But on June 10, 2008, he once again found himself in the basement courtroom of Regions Hospital listening to important strangers explain to other important strangers why it's in society's best interest to blast 140 volts of electricity through his cranium at regularly scheduled intervals. Today's hearing would decide whether the month-long court order should be allowed to expire.

One of the strangers, Dr. Peter Myers, whom Sandford had met only briefly, testified that Sandford had shown "noted improvement" since beginning ECT, in the sense that Sandford "now has the ability to remain calm." Dr. Myers also commended him for "exhibiting more organized thought patterns." However, continued the doctor, "he still remains a danger to himself and is in need of continued commitment and treatment with neuroleptic medication and electroconvulsive therapy."

Judge Warner agreed. She gave the go-ahead for three ECTs a week for up to four weeks, followed by one treatment per week for one year thereafter.

The ruling was based on solid precedent. In 1976, just as ECT was at the nadir of its popularity, a 14-year-old Minnesota boy was shocked against his and his mother's objections. The mother filed suit and went before the Minnesota Supreme Court. The resulting decision held that legally competent patients were immune from being shocked against their stated objections. Moreover, the case made clear that even incompetent patients were entitled to a court proceeding before being administered electroconvulsive therapy.

On its face, the *Price-Sheppard* decision appeared to bolster patients' self-determination—after all, the requirement for guardians to get court approval before administering the volts is one that didn't exist before.

But in practice, court-ordered ECT has been on the rise since the ruling, for a number of reasons. The ruling assumed that a committed person is—by very virtue of being committed—incompetent. Second, attaining the court order is more of a bureaucratic formality than a serious deliberation.

"I would say the court grants the order for ECT in well over 90 percent of the cases," says Doug McGuire, of the Hennepin County Commitment Defense Panel, which represents patients in the proceedings. "It's very unusual for the court not to grant the ECT request."

Mental health courts require a lower standard to the petitioner ("clear and convincing evidence") than do criminal courts ("beyond a reasonable doubt"), but more importantly, the petitioner—almost invariably a doctor, as in Sandford's case—naturally wields more credibility than a person deemed unfit to care for himself.

"One of the issues that comes up is how vigorously the person's court-appointed attorney puts forth their objections to the ECT," notes Pamela Hoopes, the lead attorney for the Minnesota Disability Law Center.

Campaign for Ray

On October 22, David Oaks was sitting in his office in Eugene, Oregon, when his phone rang.

As director of MindFreedom International, a coalition of self-described "mental human rights organizations" advocating what they call "a nonviolent revolution in mental health care," Oaks has fielded his share of strange calls. But Oaks had never heard a story like this before.

"My name is Ray Sandford," said the man on the phone. "I live in a group home in suburban Minneapolis. I'm getting electroshock treatment against my will. What do I do?"

Oaks dialed Lutheran Social Services to confirm the story. A worker familiar with Sandford's case verified that Sandford was indeed receiving court-ordered electroshock treatments. A copy of the court order confirmed it.

"I get calls all the time from people who are frightened, who are being pushed around and bullied by the mental health system," says Oaks. "But this guy has made sense the whole time. His was an extremely human response: 'I don't want it.'"

Taking up the cause, MindFreedom launched an online Campaign for Ray, with a website detailing Sandford's predicament. Oaks compiled a list of caretakers associated with Sandford—from doctors to judges to lawyers—along with their contact information, encouraging visitors to call them and demand they put an end to the treatment. In addition, MindFreedom sent out mass e-mails to its network of activists who, in turn, inundated the governor's office with phone calls.

The tactic seemed to be working. On April 15, Dr. Dean Knudson stepped aside as Sandford's psychiatrist. Eight days later, Lutheran Social Services submitted to the Ramsey County probate court a petition to resign as Sandford's guardian.

But on May 12, a knock sounded outside Sandford's door. It was his caretakers. They had come to raid his refrigerator.

"A Whole Lot Better"

The next day, Sandford emerges from his front door to a familiar sight: an idling white bus. He slowly steps forward, his four-pronged cane gripping warm asphalt.

He doesn't want to do this. He's told them repeatedly he doesn't want to do this.

He climbs inside the bus and takes a seat. A hiss sounds as the bus's brakes release.

He arrives at Mercy Medical Center and is taken to the fifth floor. An IV is inserted. Sandford is less than two minutes from undergoing his 43rd ECT when a doctor approaches him.

"Mr. Sandford, it looks like we're going to postpone today's treatment," he says. "Sorry for the inconvenience."

Unbeknownst to Sandford, his mother had, for the past 48 hours, placed dozens of calls to Mercy's ECT Unit. Her words were concise and persuasive.

"His doctor has given up on him," she told anyone who would listen. "I'm a retired nurse. And I know for a fact you cannot give ECT without a doctor's order."

It's unclear whether Sandford will have to go through with more ECT or who his new doctor will be. Marilyn and a friend are in the process of finding a psychiatrist.

As for Ray Sandford, his appraisal of last week's surprising turn is characteristically nonchalant.

"I felt a whole lot better after they told me I wouldn't have to go through with it," he says. "But I wish they would have told me earlier, instead of having to go through all the trouble. They knew I didn't want to do this."

> *"If patients with schizophrenia don't perceive themselves as having a mental illness and they receive medication that they don't perceive as beneficial, the chances of treatment adherence and successful outcomes diminish tremendously."*

Schizophrenia Can Be Successfully Treated with Medication

Joseph P. McEvoy

Joseph P. McEvoy is an associate professor of psychiatry at Duke University. In the following viewpoint, McEvoy contends that the best chances of recovery from schizophrenia depend on early treatment and adherence to medication. McEvoy claims that the longer antipsychotic drugs are delayed, the condition will become more persistent and resistant to treatment, and the patient's ability to work or function are more likely to be impaired. Therefore, practitioners must help patients recognize their illness and that medication improves their daily lives.

As you read, consider the following questions:

1. What limits people with schizophrenia from seeking and adhering to treatment?

2. What research does the author cite to support the argument that antipsychotic drugs are effective in treating schizophrenia?

3. What practical evidence can care providers offer patients to encourage adherence to medication?

Schizophrenia is a devastating illness, taking a tremendous toll on patients, families, employers, and communities. Early and effective intervention is vital. In this article, Joseph P. McEvoy, MD, shares his thoughts on the importance of responding to the early signs of psychosis and suggests ways to help patients with adherence to antipsychotic medication treatment. Dr. McEvoy is an associate professor of psychiatry at Duke University Medical Center and deputy director at John Umstead Hospital in Butner, North Carolina.

[ILLUSTRATION OMITTED]

With the onset of schizophrenia, patients need reliable, consistent control of their symptoms to begin to rebuild their lives. The early and effective treatment of schizophrenia can make a significant difference in the long-term recovery of most patients. (1)

The improved understanding of schizophrenia as a neurobiologic disorder and the recognition that intervention is needed as early as possible following the onset of illness offer the potential to optimize long-term treatment outcomes. Persons experiencing symptoms of schizophrenia may have limited insight into the nature of the illness, thus limiting their ability to seek and adhere to treatment. Therefore, it is important for those who play key roles in the development of young adults, such as teachers, counselors, and physicians, to recognize the symptoms of schizophrenia and help patients seek treatment. (2)

Family members and friends may believe that the individual is going through a growing phase or trying out a new philosophy of life rather than experiencing the early stages of a mental illness. For family members, the diagnosis of schizophrenia is further complicated because the onset of illness is usually in the late teens or early 20s, when young people may harbor ideas that may be perceived as unconventional. When these seemingly odd ideas are accompanied by a reversal in normal sleep cycles, withdrawal from social activities to spend more time alone, neglect of normal hygiene and self-care, or loss of jobs with ill-defined attribution of persecution or maltreatment, family members and other adults should consider seeking medical attention for the individual.

Unfortunately, there are often delays between the appearance of initial psychotic episodes and the correct diagnosis and treatment, which can result in decreased responsiveness to treatment and diminished social and occupational functioning. By identifying and treating psychotic episodes soon after onset, it may be possible to limit the damage, reduce recovery time, and help patients resume daily activities and social functioning. (3)

Early Negative Outcomes

A longer duration of untreated psychosis prior to starting therapy with antipsychotic medications is correlated with more significant, persistent psychopathology and poorer functional outcomes, according to recent studies. (4) Therefore, to prevent deterioration in the quality of patients' lives, it is extremely important to identify individuals experiencing the onset of schizophrenia as early as possible in workplaces, schools, or physician offices.

Brain imaging studies suggest that many individuals experience a loss of brain volume following their initial psychotic

New Discoveries May Enhance Medications' Effectiveness

New research has discovered that when there is an abnormal relationship between dopamine and glutamate—two signaling chemicals in the brain—the result is often psychosis.

The study offers a new angle in understanding psychotic symptoms, possibly leading to more effective drugs for schizophrenia. . . .

Current drugs used to treat schizophrenia hamper the effects of dopamine in the brain. These drugs, however, are not successful in all patients, and often carry harmful side effects.

The new findings unveil the fact that the high levels of dopamine found in people with psychotic symptoms actually occur as a result of changes in another brain chemical, glutamate. . . .

This research shows that if a drug were to interfere with glutamate signals in the brain, psychotic symptoms in people with schizophrenia may be prevented.

Traci Pedersen,
"Understanding Glutamate and Psychosis Offers Hope
for Schizophrenia," PsychCentral, *October 2, 2010.*

episode. Even if persons with schizophrenia receive treatment immediately after onset, they still may lose brain volume, according to the latest studies. (5)

Figure 1 is from a longitudinal follow-up study of patients experiencing a first psychotic episode and matched control subjects, conducted by Lieberman et al. (5) The x-axis reflects the time in days between the baseline and follow-up brain scans. The y-axis reflects change in ventricular volume from baseline to follow-up. The greater the number, the greater the increase in ventricular volume and, consequently, the greater the loss of brain tissue volume. Control subjects, depicted by the diamonds, show no change in ventricular volume irrespective of the time between scans. The patients who had good therapeutic outcomes, depicted by the squares, similarly show no changes in ventricular volume. However, those patients who had poor therapeutic outcomes (triangles) show consistent increases in ventricular volume, and the longer the duration of follow-up, the greater the loss of brain tissue volume.

Finally, recent studies show that patients who do lose brain volume clearly have a worse prognosis for recovery than those who do not. The longer antipsychotic medication is delayed, the more persistent and treatment-resistant the psychopathology may become, meaning that patients are more likely to suffer long-term functional impairments such as inability to sustain employment. (4)

Unfortunately, even after the early stages of the illness are treated, there is a high risk for psychotic exacerbations, especially if patients do not believe they need treatment or the treatment is incompletely effective. These individuals often do not want to view themselves as ill or needing treatment. (6)

[FIGURE 1 OMITTED]

In addition to a lack of insight, an ineffective response to an initially selected antipsychotic can lead to distress or apathy and ultimately, discontinuation of treatment. (7) Moreover, without effective treatment, most patients will experience a diminution in the quality of their lives as they become increasingly impaired. These patients may engage in progressively unusual behavior that makes it difficult for them to maintain normal relationships at home, at school, at work, and in the community. Some patients may even attempt suicide. (5)

Early and Effective Treatment

Patients who experience negative outcomes from their early treatment are less likely to adhere to their antipsychotic medication regimen; those whose symptoms are rapidly and effectively controlled are more likely to adhere to their prescribed medications. (7) Therefore, it is important for practitioners to carefully monitor the patient's response to medication once treatment of psychotic episodes has been initiated.

Polypharmacy often complicates treatment adherence and increases the likelihood of adverse events. In treating schizophrenia, it may thus be preferable to switch rather than add antipsychotics to augment response. Expert consensus guidelines published in 2003 recommend that practitioners wait three to five weeks prior to switching to another therapy. (8) However, recent evidence suggests that the effects of most antipsychotic agents can be recognized within two weeks of treatment and, therefore, a practitioner may consider the decision to switch earlier than the recommended three to five weeks. (9, 10)

In a 2005 study by Leucht et al, acutely psychotic patients treated with an effective antipsychotic showed a 40 to 50% reduction over time in their mean Brief Psychiatric Rating Scale (BPRS) total scores (figure 2). (9) This improvement was "front-loaded." There was an 18 to 19% improvement during the first week of treatment, and an additional 12 to 13% improvement during the second week (for a total of 30 to 32% improvement during the first two weeks). The next two weeks of treatment (weeks three and four) brought only an additional 11 to 12% improvement. Although further gradual improvement accrued during the ensuing months, the rate of improvement was much less than during the initial two weeks.

[FIGURE 2 OMITTED]

Treatment Adherence and Avoiding Relapse

Additional studies are needed to determine the most effective treatments for initial episodes of schizophrenia. However, it seems clear that those individuals who experience better therapeutic responses or perceive early improvements in their condition after their first psychotic episode are much more likely to adhere to their medication regimen and, not surprisingly, fare better in long-term recovery. (11)

Two key influencers that predict whether patients will give up on their medication are lack of insight into the need for treatment and lack of perceived therapeutic response. In a recent large 18-month study, (11) the second most common reason patients discontinued their medication was that they didn't perceive it was improving their condition. Perhaps counter to common expectations, the influence of negative side effects was a less important trigger of discontinuation in this study. These findings support the view that a switch in antipsychotic medication should be considered sooner rather than later if satisfactory improvement is not seen.

If patients with schizophrenia don't perceive themselves as having a mental illness and they receive medication that they don't perceive as beneficial, the chances of treatment adherence and successful outcomes diminish tremendously. (12) To optimize adherence and, ultimately, better outcomes, practitioners should encourage patients to incorporate their medicines into their daily routines. Setting up practical behavioral routines will have more useful effects on adherence than abstract discussions about the importance of adherence in relapse prevention. (13) Examples of behavioral routines include having a daily pillbox in a prominent location where it will be seen every day, and linking medication ingestion to an event that happens around the same time every day, such as waking up in the morning, having dinner, or going to bed at night.

Connecting with Patients

In addition, when working with individuals with schizophrenia, it is important to maintain consistent, sympathetic contact with patients and family members. (14) Patients with schizophrenia may have limited social lives with few personal connections, and they often respond well to physicians they perceive as truly interested in their lives.

To treat individuals with schizophrenia successfully, it is also important to understand that these patients may have impaired verbal learning. (15) For this reason, adherence is best encouraged by providing practical evidence that medication is improving patients' lives—for example, patients' subjective experience that they are sleeping better, or that they are experiencing less misery, anxiety, or discomfort, is more compelling than a lecture about the importance of medication in preventing relapse.

It is better to avoid traditional adherence strategies that review the medical nature of schizophrenia and discuss the importance of treatment and the necessity of adherence. Such approaches are based on explicit memory, which allows us to remember lecture points or the rules of a game, and patients with schizophrenia have severely impaired explicit memory. (16) However, these patients have intact implicit memory, which is the faculty that helps us get the hang of a game by playing it. It's far more useful to develop the habit of taking prescribed medications regularly than to listen to fluent verbal explanations of why it is important to take them.

Since patients with schizophrenia have much better implicit than explicit memories, employment programs that immediately place them in jobs with the support of on-site coaches have been much more successful than programs that rely on verbal training. Traditional vocational rehabilitation programs, therefore, which stress classroom learning about proper behavior in the workplace, are usually not a good fit for persons with schizophrenia. For example, handing out employee manuals to individuals with schizophrenia and expecting them to understand the rules of the workplace may not yield desired goals. It is much better to have an on-site coach who encourages these individuals, shows them how to do the necessary tasks well by working with them, and provides pragmatic support. (17)

Summary

It is extremely important to treat schizophrenia as soon as possible after the onset. (14) With delay in effective treatment, patients may be at increased risk for brain volume loss with adverse implications for long-term treatment outcomes.

Providers should not try to "instruct" patients with schizophrenia, who often have impaired verbal learning abilities, about the necessity of adhering to their medication regimen, but instead should try to demonstrate that the treatment can effectively improve their lives. To this end, it is crucial to find a medication at a dose that relieves psychotic and affective psychopathology as quickly as possible. To optimize treatment adherence, it seems more practical for providers to help patients with schizophrenia feel subjectively better and recognize improvement than to impress them with the logic of the argument for taking medications. (18)

In treating schizophrenia, physicians also should be involved and accessible to patients and caregivers. Providers should treat their patients with respect, express their viewpoint succinctly and consistently, and make clear that the betterment of the patient is their goal.

Notes

1. Wyatt RJ. Neuroleptics and the natural course of schizophrenia. Schizophr Bull 1991; 17:325-51.
2. Anthony WA. Recovery from mental illness: The guiding vision of the mental health service system in the 1990s. Psychosoc Rehabil J 1993; 16 (4): 11-23.
3. Lehman AF, Lieberman JA, Dixon LB, et al; American Psychiatric Association; Steering Committee on Practice Guide-

lines. Practice guideline for the treatment of patients with chizophrenia, second edition. Am J Psychiatry 2004; 161 (suppl 2): 1-56.

4. Perkins DO, Gu H, Boteva K, Lieberman JA. Relationship between duration of untreated psychosis and outcome in first-episode schizophrenia: A critical review and meta-analysis. Am J Psychiatry 2005; 162:1785-1804.

5. Lieberman J, Chakos M, Wu H, et al. Longitudinal study of brain morphology in first episode schizophrenia. Biol Psychiatry 2001; 49:487-99.

6. McEvoy JP, Johnson J, Perkins D, et al. Insight in first-episode psychosis. Psychol Med 2006; 36:1385-93.

7. Liu-Seifert H, Adams DH, Kinon BJ. Discontinuation of treatment of schizophrenic patients is driven by poor symptom response: A pooled post-hoc analysis of four atypical antipsychotic drugs. BMC Med 2005; 3:21.

8. Kane JM, Leucht S, Carpenter D, Docherty JP; Expert Consensus Panel for Optimizing Pharmacologic Treatment of Psychotic Disorders. The expert consensus guideline series. Optimizing pharmacologic treatment of psychotic disorders. Introduction: Methods, commentary, and summary. J Clin Psychiatry 2003; 64 (suppl 12): 5-19.

9. Leucht S, Busch R, Hamann J, et al. Early-onset hypothesis of antipsychotic drug action: A hypothesis tested, confirmed and extended. Biol Psychiatry 2005; 57:1543-9.

10. Agid O, Kapur S, Arenovich T, Zipursky RB. Delayed-onset hypothesis of antipsychotic action: A hypothesis tested and rejected. Arch Gen Psychiatry 2003; 60:1228-35.

11. Lieberman JA, Stroup TS, McEvoy JP, et al; Clinical Antipsychotic Trials of Intervention Effectiveness (CATIE) Investigators. Effectiveness of antipsychotic drugs in patients with chronic schizophrenia. N Engl J Med 2005; 353:1209-23.

12. Perkins DO, Johnson JL, Hamer RM, et al, HGDH Research Group. Predictors of antipsychotic medication ad-

herence in patients recovering from a first psychotic episode. Schizophr Res 2006; 83:53-63.

13. Boczkowski JA, Zeichner A, DeSanto N. Neuroleptic compliance among chronic schizophrenic outpatients: An intervention outcome report. J Consult Clin Psychol 1985; 53:666-71.

14. Lamberti JS. Seven keys to relapse prevention in schizophrenia. J Psychiatr Pract 2001; 7:253-9.

15. Saykin AJ, Shtasel DL, Gur RE, et al. Neuropsychological deficits in neuroleptic naive patients with first-episode schizophrenia. Arch Gen Psychiatry 1994; 51:124-31.

16. Huron C, Danion JM, Giacomoni F, et al. Impairment of recognition memory with, but not without, conscious recollection in schizophrenia. Am J Psychiatry 1995; 152:1737-42.

17. Lehman AF, Goldberg R, Dixon LB, et al. Improving employment outcomes for persons with severe mental illnesses. Arch Gen Psychiatry 2002; 59:165-72.

18. Perkins R. What constitutes success? The relative priority of service users' and clinicians' views of mental health services. Br J Psychiatry 2001; 179:9-10.

| *"The human experience of 'psychosis' can be helped without recourse to the use of antipsychotic medication."*

Schizophrenia Can Be Successfully Treated Without Medication

Tim Calton

Based in England, Tim Calton is a psychiatrist, research fellow at the United Kingdom's Institute of Mental Health, and special lecturer at the University of Nottingham. In the following viewpoint, Calton argues that nondrug approaches to treating schizophrenia can be beneficial and advantageous. Historical evidence, the author claims, shows that support and care emphasizing respect and interpersonal relationships have allowed people with schizophrenia to function in daily life. Moreover, studies reveal that such approaches have produced better outcomes—such as more participants living independently and experiencing fewer readmissions—and alternatives to antipsychotic medication deserve reconsideration, he states.

As you read, consider the following questions:

1. How does the importance granted to medication affect psychiatric treatment, in the author's opinion?

2. What characterized the program at the Soteria House, according to the author?

3. What does Calton contend were the benefits of "need adapted" treatment?

Over two hundred years ago medical psychiatry planted its standard within the realm of the human experience of 'madness', quickly becoming the dominant paradigm. Other ways of understanding and tending to mental distress were suffocated or retreated to the margins. Psychiatry's success in creating and disseminating knowledge about those forms of life which get described as 'madness', 'psychosis', or 'schizophrenia', quickly becomes apparent when surveying the first National Institute for [Health and] Clinical Excellence (NICE) guidelines for the treatment of people diagnosed with schizophrenia.

This document, a synopsis of so-called 'best practice' in the clinical treatment of 'schizophrenia' within the NHS [National Health Service], clearly states that antipsychotic drugs are necessary in the treatment of an acute episode, a mandate not extended to psychosocial interventions.

Last month [March 2009] we had the updated guidelines. They do appear somewhat more balanced (stating that cognitive-behavioural psychotherapy should be offered alongside medication), although important semantic emphases remain (such as the fact that clinicians need only 'discuss' alternative therapies, not necessarily offer them). The importance granted medication, at the expense of other ways of understanding and helping with mental distress, reflects the tendency for medical psychiatry to see aspects of the vast and complex realm of human experience as mere disease.

Although the NICE guidelines carry a powerful political imprimatur they reflect the deep but extremely narrow tradition of biomedical research into madness; research which would have us believe that the only way to 'get better' and 'stay well' are to take antipsychotic medication, for life if necessary.

The question remains, however, as to whether it is possible to help people experiencing 'psychosis' without recourse to antipsychotic medication? Such a question might provoke a range of immediate and urgent responses depending on your sociopolitical context, life history and experience. One way of mediating this array of responses would be to scrutinise 'the evidence' supporting the use of no or minimal medication approaches to the treatment of 'psychosis'/'schizophrenia'.

A Wealth of Historical Evidence

There is certainly a wealth of historical evidence supporting a nonmedical approach to madness ranging from Geel, the city in Belgium where the 'mad' lived with local families, receiving support and care that allowed them to function in the 'normal' social world despite the emotional distress some experienced, to the so-called Moral Treatment developed at the York Retreat by William Tuke towards the end of the eighteenth century, which advocated peace, respect, and dignity in all relationships, and emphasised the importance of maintaining usual social activities, work and exercise. These approaches, predicated as they were on a gentle and humane engagement with the vagaries of human experience at the limits, and invoking respect, dignity, collective responsibility, and an emphasis on interpersonal relationships as guiding principles, have much to tell contemporary biomedical psychiatry.

In the modern era, nonmedical attempts to understand and tend to 'psychosis' have coalesced into a tradition counterposed to the biomedical orthodoxy. The richest seam of evidence within this tradition is that relating to Soteria House,

Discontinuing Medication

It is possible that certain persons with schizophrenia can discontinue their medication at some time. Some research has suggested that as many as one-third of all people who have an episode of schizophrenia may not have another serious episode, even without medication. A reasonable rule of thumb is that a patient who has been compliant with his or her medication regimen and completely symptom free for 1 year could try to discontinue the medication under the supervision of a medical professional. Generally, the medication is reduced gradually, with each new reduced dosage maintained for at least a month. Our own research study has suggested that 2 to 4 weeks off medication is the crucial time for relapse in a patient who has been asymptomatic on medication. As a result, many people can test to see if they still require their medication and can know in a month or so after the final dose. After medication is discontinued, careful monitoring of the person for warning signs of impending relapse will also be required for at least another year.

Richard S.E. Keefe and Philip D. Harvey,
Understanding Schizophrenia: A Guide to the New Research on Causes and Treatment. *New York: The Free Press, 1994.*

the project developed by Loren Mosher and colleagues in San Francisco during the early 1970s. Here, people diagnosed with schizophrenia could live in a suburban house staffed with nonprofessionals who would spend time 'being' with them in an attempt to try and secure shared meanings and understandings of their subjective experience.

Antipsychotic medication was marginalised, being considered a barrier to the project of understanding the other, and was only ever taken from a position of informed and voluntary choice. Arguably the most radical aspect of the Soteria project was the emphasis given to building a case across many different rhetorical levels, including the scientific/evidential. Subjected to a randomised controlled trial in comparison to 'treatment as usual' (TAU—hospitalisation and medication), with follow-up assessments at six weeks and two years, it proved at least as effective as TAU with some specific advantages in terms of significantly greater improvements in global psychopathology and composite outcome, significantly more participants living independently, and significantly fewer readmissions. A Swiss iteration of Soteria reported similar results and suggested these could be achieved at no greater fiscal cost than TAU, whilst a recent systematic review of all the evidence pertaining to Soteria confirmed both claims.

More evidence supporting the use of nonmedical approaches to helping people diagnosed with 'psychosis'/ 'schizophrenia' has emerged from Scandinavia and the USA. In the former, so-called 'Need Adapted' treatment, an approach which places great emphasis on interpersonal relationships and striving after meaning, whilst decentring medication, beating it as merely one of a plurality of interventions, is associated with people spending less time in hospital, experiencing fewer 'psychotic' symptoms, being more likely to hold down a job, and taking much less antipsychotic medication. In the latter, evidence from an innovative series of research projects conducted in the 1970s suggests not only that people diagnosed with 'schizophrenia' can recover without the use of antipsychotic medication when exposed to a nurturing and tolerant therapeutic environment, but also that antipsychotic medication may not be the treatment of choice, at least for certain people, if the goal is long-term improvement.

Overcoming the Biomedical Bias

To conclude then, it seems appropriate, given the evidence, to claim that the human experience of 'psychosis' can be helped without recourse to the use of antipsychotic medication. The research cited above does not appear to have been considered in the current NICE guidelines (presumably because of the small number of studies undertaken using minimal or no medication approaches), though may well be incorporated into the next iteration. This should happen because the lack of any meaningful idea of choice with regard to treatment for people diagnosed with 'psychosis'/'schizophrenia' in the UK [United Kingdom] is abundantly apparent; a state of affairs that may not be sustainable given recent pronouncements on patient choice.

We must remember, honour and reiterate these alternative traditions of thought and practice if we are to overcome the extant biomedical hegemony.

| "Cognitive Therapy . . . has been shown to be an effective treatment for many, many psychiatric disorders, psychological problems, and medical conditions with psychological components."

Cognitive Behavioral Therapy Is a Valuable Treatment

Judith Beck, as told to Judy Madewell and Michael F. Shaughnessy

Judith Beck is director of the Beck Institute for Cognitive Therapy and Research and psychiatry professor at the University of Pennsylvania. Judy Madewell is a clinical counselor in New Mexico. Michael F. Shaughnessy is a special education professor at Eastern New Mexico University. In the following viewpoint, Beck discusses the benefits of cognitive behavioral therapy (sometimes called cognitive therapy) with Madewell and Shaughnessy. According to Beck, cognitive behavioral therapy is based on the premise that distorted or dysfunctional thinking affects mood or behavior; treatment is designed to teach patients the skills to counter these patterns, evaluate negative thoughts, and solve cur-

Judith Beck, Judy Madewell, and Michael F. Shaughnessy, "An Interview with Judith Beck About Cognitive Therapy," *North American Journal of Psychology*, 2009. Copyright © 2009 *North American Journal of Psychology*. Reprinted with permission.

rent problems. She points out that patients with clear-cut issues such as depression and anxiety are ideal candidates for cognitive behavioral therapy.

As you read, consider the following questions:

1. As told by Beck, what happens during a session of cognitive behavioral therapy?

2. What problems arise for professionals who practice cognitive behavioral therapy, in Beck's opinion?

3. What role does medication play in cognitive behavioral therapy, in Beck's view?

Judith S. Beck is the director of the Beck Institute for Cognitive Therapy and Research in suburban Philadelphia and clinical associate professor of psychology in psychiatry at the University of Pennsylvania, where she teaches residents. Dr. Beck currently divides her time between administration, supervision and teaching, clinical work, program development, research and writing. She is a consultant for several NIMH [National Institute of Mental Health] research studies and has presented hundreds of seminars and workshops nationally and internationally on cognitive therapy for a wide variety of psychiatric disorders. She authored *Cognitive Therapy: Basics and Beyond*, which has been translated into 20 languages. Her other books include *Cognitive Therapy for Challenging Problems: What to Do When the Basics Don't Work, Oxford Textbook of Psychotherapy, Cognitive Therapy of Personality Disorders, The Beck Diet Solution* and *The Beck Diet Solution Weight Loss Workbook*, a cognitive therapy approach to weight loss and maintenance. Dr. Deck is a past president of the Academy of Cognitive Therapy.

NAJP [North American Journal of Psychology]: There is great diversity of applications for CBT [cognitive behavioral therapy]. At what times would you say "use CBT only"? For what disorders would you not recommend CBT?

JB [Judith Beck]: Cognitive Therapy (sometimes synonymous with CBT) has been shown to be an effective treatment for many, many psychiatric disorders, psychological problems, and medical conditions with psychological components (you can find a list at www.academyofct.org). I look at the question this way: If I had asthma, I would first want my doctors to prescribe the treatment that research shows is most effective. If that didn't help, or didn't help enough, I'd want them to add to or change the treatment, again based on research findings. CBT should not be used as a frontline treatment when research shows that other treatments are more effective, either in the short-run or in preventing relapse, in the long-run. . . .

NAJP: Your web page refers to a Forbes *magazine article entitled "Patient Fix Thyself." Does this title imply that individuals can solve mental health issues without seeking therapy?*

JB: Research shows that some people with problems such as mild depression can resolve their difficulties through bibliotherapy or exercise. But most people can't. The reference to "fixing" oneself is associated with the psycho-educational component of CBT. We not only help people solve their problems and respond to their dysfunctional thinking and behavior in order to feel better—but we also teach them how to implement these techniques themselves, for the rest of their lives, to prevent or reduce relapse.

NAJP: What tools does the average person need to self-administer Cognitive Therapy?

JB: There are a number of good books for consumers about Cognitive Therapy; people can visit www.academyofct .org and click on "Consumers." The list is divided into various problems and disorders, and age groups.

NAJP: What problems most often arise in practicing Cognitive Therapy as a professional?

JB: Although the theory behind cognitive therapy is consistent across disorders, mental health professionals need to learn the specific cognitive formulation and specific treatment strategies for each disorder, and then apply this knowledge to each unique individual, taking into consideration his or her gender, age, culture, stage of life, history, and so on. The treatment for depression, for example, focuses on negative ideas about the self, the world, and the future. Emphasizing these kinds of cognitions, however, is unlikely to help patients with panic disorder, who need to test their fears about the catastrophe they predict will arise if their physiological symptoms intensify.

NAJP: In what ways do you see the roles of therapists changing?

JB: Therapists are finally being held more accountable, especially by managed care companies, for the progress of their patients and are increasingly being asked to use treatments that research has shown to be effective.

NAJP: What do you think of Dialectical Behavior Therapy (DBT)? Are there times when DBT would be more efficacious than CBT?

JB: There has not been sufficient research to answer the question of efficacy. Both treatment modalities have been demonstrated to be effective in treating borderline personality disorder. Although their underlying theoretical rationales differ, they use many of the same techniques. CBT has a much stronger emphasis on helping patients change their dysfunctional thoughts and beliefs, along with modifying their emotional responses and behavior.

A Research-Based Treatment

NAJP: Cognitive Therapy has enjoyed phenomenal clinical success in numerous studies. Had your family any idea that Cognitive Therapy would get this big?

JB: When my father developed Cognitive Therapy as a treatment for depression in the early 1960s, he says he didn't realize at the time that it would have applicability to any other disorder. But then he and I and colleagues around the world began to apply the cognitive model to other psychiatric (and later medical) problems. We found that a specific cognitive formulation could be developed for each disorder or problem (and that accurate cognitive conceptualizations of individual patients could be devised, across disorders), to enable them to develop effective treatments. Then research was conducted to test the efficacy of treatment for each disorder. . . .

NAJP: What exactly is cognitive therapy?

JB: Cognitive therapy (cognitive refers to thinking) is a research-based treatment. Therapy sessions are usually structured and oriented toward helping patients solve their current problems. In the context of solving these problems, patients learn problem-solving, thinking, and behavioral skills that they use not only during treatment but also in the future, to stay well. An important part of treatment is helping patients learn how to evaluate the validity and usefulness of their negative thoughts and how to respond to them in a realistic way. When they do so, they feel better and are able to behave more functionally.

Treatment is time-sensitive and is usually much shorter than other psychotherapies since a major goal is to teach patients to be their own therapist. For this reason, cognitive therapy not only helps people get better, but also to stay better. Many patients with straightforward problems of depression or anxiety, for example, are treated in just six to twelve sessions.

The Theory Behind Cognitive Therapy

NAJP: What is the theory or philosophy behind cognitive therapy?

JB: In a nutshell, cognitive therapy is based on the idea that people in distress often have distorted (incorrect) and/or dysfunctional (unhelpful) thinking. This thinking has a negative impact on their mood, behavior, and often, physiology. For example, Dena (not her real name) was depressed. She perceived that her friend, Emily, was irritated when Dena was a few minutes late arriving for lunch. Dena thought, "I can't believe I kept her waiting. That was so bad. She's probably really angry at me. She probably won't want to get together with me again." Dena didn't even think to evaluate the validity of her thinking. She just accepted her thoughts as true. But when people are in distress, their ideas are often untrue or largely untrue. I asked Dena, "What's the evidence that your friend was angry—or stayed angry? In the scheme of things, how bad is it to make the mistake of being a few minutes late. How do you know that your friend doesn't want to see you again?"

When I helped Dena evaluate her thinking, she concluded, "I guess it wasn't so terrible that I was late. Even if Emily was irritated at the moment, we actually had a good time at lunch. There's no evidence that she won't want to get together again." When Dena viewed the situation more realistically, she felt better and was able to act in a more helpful way. After our session, she called Emily and arranged to have coffee with her the following weekend.

Another patient, Rick (not his real name), was quite anxious about taking his children on an outing, because he was thinking, "What if something bad happens? What if I can't handle it? If I'm not on my guard every moment and on the lookout for danger, I'll be responsible if something does happen." As a result, Rick was fearful, experienced uncomfortable physiological arousal, and was so hyper-vigilant for harm that he couldn't enjoy himself at the park and just have fun with his children. Had he evaluated his thinking, he might have concluded, "Accidents rarely occur at the park. The potential benefits to my kids and me far outweigh whatever very small risk there is. If I take reasonable precautions (set ground rules for the kids and keep an eye on them as they play on the playground equipment), I can minimize whatever small risk there might be. In order to avert all potential harm to the kids, I'd have to make them stay in bed all day, which wouldn't be good for them, anyway. If something does happen, I know what to do. I can call [my friend] on my cell phone or I can drive the kids to the hospital. I'm not helpless." Once Rick was able to consistently respond to his thinking in this way, his anxiety decreased tremendously.

As another example, I have found that people who struggle with losing weight or maintaining their weight loss also have a lot of unhelpful thinking. They often think differently from people who have never had a weight problem. For example, they tend to think, "Hunger is bad. If I'm hungry, I should eat." "If I crave a food, there's nothing I can do, I'll end up eating it so I might as well give in and eat it now." "It's okay to eat this food I hadn't planned to have because I'm stressed, I'm happy, it's a special occasion, it's free, no one is watching, it will boost my energy, I'm going to exercise later, it looks really good, I can't resist it, everyone else is eating it." "It's unfair if I can't eat like [non-dieters]." "Dieting should be easy and short-term." These kinds of thoughts interfere with dieters' ability to follow their eating plan but once they learn to effectively respond to these thoughts, they can be successful.

Setting an Agenda

NAJP: What happens during a typical cognitive therapy session?

JB: First we do a mood check to find out how patients have been feeling since their last session. We want to make sure that the treatment is working. We also ask, "What happened between last session and today (both positive and negative) that is important for me to know? What's coming up before I see you again that might be important for us to talk about today? What self-help assignments did you do and what did you learn from them?"

Then we set an agenda by asking, "What problem or problems do you want my help in solving today?" We prioritize the problems on the agenda and start discussing the first one. We ask questions to help us understand what the difficulty is, why it arose, and whether distorted thinking or behavior was involved in the initiation and/or maintenance of the problem. In the context of the discussion, we spend some time problem-solving and some time helping patients evaluate the validity and utility of their dysfunctional (unhelpful) thinking, and we teach patients cognitive and behavioral skills they need to solve the problem. We collaboratively decide what it might be helpful for patients to do between sessions and what they may need to remind themselves so they can have a better week. Then we ask for feedback. "What did you think about the session? Anything that bothered you? Anything you want to do differently next time?"

A Highly Collaborative Process

NAJP: What about medication? What role does it play in cognitive therapy?

JB: Research shows that cognitive therapy alone is more effective than medication for some disorders, that they are roughly equivalent for other disorders, and that the combination of the two is better for yet other disorders. Cognitive therapy is a highly collaborative process, and therapists respect patients' preferences. When patients have serious mental illness such as schizophrenia or bipolar disorder, however, therapists will spend time helping patients evaluate the advantages and disadvantages of taking medication and explain that therapy alone is unlikely to be effective enough.

NAJP: Are there any CT/ CBT computer-assisted educational programs that can help clients or patients?

JB: Michael, there are a few but I don't have a comprehensive list, and I'd rather not endorse the couple I know about over ones I don't know about.

NAJP: What question have we neglected to ask?

JB: An important question is, "How do I find a cognitive therapist?" Unfortunately, many psychotherapists these days call themselves cognitive therapists but have not received suffi-

"Rather than fighting the feeling attached to a behavior, a person can observe oneself as having the feeling but still act."

Acceptance and Commitment Therapy Is a Beneficial Treatment

Claudia Dewane

Claudia Dewane is the founder of Clinical Support Associates, an organization for social workers, and she is senior lecturer at the School of Social Work at Temple University. In the following viewpoint, Dewane contends that acceptance and commitment therapy—wherein an individual can take action without altering or getting rid of a feeling first—is more effective than cognitive behavioral therapy. With the former, the emphasis is on changing behaviors regardless of the associated feeling and accepting that suffering is part of life, Dewane explains. Acceptance and commitment therapy is suited as a therapeutic tool for a variety of problems, the author states, from traumatic childhood abuse to relationship conflicts.

Claudia Dewane, "The ABCs of ACT—Acceptance and Commitment Therapy," *Social Work Today*, vol. 8, no. 5, September–October 2008. Copyright © 2008 *Social Work Today*. Reproduced by permission.

As you read, consider the following questions:

1. What example of a "verbal and cognitive shift" does Dewane provide?

2. How does acceptance and commitment therapy examine strategies that have not worked, as described by Dewane?

3. What is the "self as context," in Dewane's words?

*C*lient: *"I want to change, BUT I am too anxious."*

Social worker: *"You want to change, AND you are anxious about it."*

This subtle verbal and cognitive shift is the essence of acceptance and commitment therapy (ACT). It suggests that a person can take action without first changing or eliminating feelings. Rather than fighting the feeling attached to a behavior, a person can observe oneself as having the feeling but still act. Acceptance-based approaches postulate that instead of opting for change alone, the most effective approach may be to accept and change. The importance of acceptance has long been recognized in the Serenity Prayer.

As one of the postmodern behavioral approaches, ACT is being evaluated as another short-term intervention in a variety of populations seen by social workers.

Evolution of ACT

Psychodynamic approaches that emphasize insight imply that a change in attitude will most likely result in a change in behavior. In contrast, pure behavioral approaches suggest that altering behavior does not demand a change in attitude. However, changing a behavior may eventually result in a change in attitude or emotion. Focusing on changing behavior regardless of accompanying emotion is the emphasis.

Taking behaviorism a step further, ACT suggests that both behavior and emotion can exist simultaneously and independently. Acceptance has been described as the "missing link in traditional behavior therapy." ACT is part of a larger movement in the behavioral and cognitive realm, which includes the mindfulness approaches.

[Researcher S.C.] Hayes has been credited as the founder of ACT as a contextual approach to treatment. He explores the paradoxes of context, such as separating words and actions, and distinguishing clients' sense of self from their thoughts and behavior. For example, when a person doesn't go to work because he or she is anxious about a confrontation with his or her boss, it is conceivable (and encouraged) that the individual can go to work while feeling anxious. Showing clients that they can live with anxiety and eliminate the control that contexts exert is a major goal of therapy. Those familiar with rational emotive behavioral therapy will recognize this approach as consistent with verbal rule governance ("injunctions").

ACT is born from the behavioral school of therapy. However, behavior therapy is divided into three generations: traditional behaviorism, cognitive behavioral therapy (CBT), and the current "third generation" or contextual approaches to behavior. This third wave of behaviorism has an existential bent in its premise that suffering is a basic characteristic of human life and represents a dramatic change from traditional behaviorism and CBT due to the inclusion of acceptance and mindfulness-based interventions. The third wave, which also includes dialectical behavior therapy and mindfulness-based cognitive therapy, broadens attention to the psychological, contextual, and experiential world of its constituents.

The belief behind ACT is that a more fulfilled life can be attained by overcoming negative thoughts and feelings. The goal of ACT is to help clients consistently choose to act effectively (concrete behaviors as defined by their values) in the presence of difficult or disruptive "private" (cognitive or psychological) events. The acronym ACT has also been used to describe what takes place in therapy: accept the effects of life's hardships, choose directional values, and take action.

Theoretical Base

Social work literature about ACT is limited. As is typical of much of social work's derivative knowledge base, the literature from the fields of psychology and social psychology contribute to understanding ACT and its application to social work practice. The literature on ACT dates back to the early 1980s but, more recently, has been evidencing empirical promise.

ACT is a unique psychotherapeutic approach based on relational frame theory (RFT). RFT questions the context in which rational change strategies exist based on principles of behavior analysis. By examining the interactions that people have with their natural and social environments (contexts), RFT provides an understanding of the power of verbal behavior and language. The theory holds that much of what we call psychopathology is the result of the human tendency to avoid negatively evaluated private events (what we think and feel). ACT highlights the ways that language traps clients into attempts to wage war against their internal lives. Clients learn to recontextualize and accept these private events, develop greater clarity about personal values, and commit to needed behavior change. For social workers, this philosophy is best understood as "person in environment," with the added variable of how language is used to interpret and direct those environments.

Process

The core of ACT is a change in both internal (self-talk) and external (action) verbal behavior. Simply observing oneself having feelings and recognizing and accepting that feelings are a natural outgrowth of circumstances is freeing. Clients have feelings about feelings (e.g., they might be ashamed of being anxious, angry, or sad). ACT says that fighting emotions makes them worse "If you can't accept the feeling for now, you will be stuck with it, but if you can, you can change your world so you will not have that feeling later."

[Researcher M.A.] Mattaini explains that ACT does not mean we ask clients to accept every situation (e.g., abusive relationships), but that some circumstances should ultimately be accepted (i.e., physical reality or historical events), should be accepted for now, should be accepted with expectation of eventual change, or should be changed now.

For example, if a client is disturbed by memories of past events, he or she must accept that the event occurred; accompanying feelings can eventually be diminished. This concept is reminiscent of social work's strengths perspective in which [researcher D.] Saleebey advises that one can accept the verdict yet defy the sentence.

Reminiscent of the Serenity Prayer, Mattaini cautions that the initial work is to identify areas that can and cannot be changed. Physical handicaps and past trauma are examples of things that cannot be changed and are best accepted.

ACT focuses on a shift from the content of experience to the context of experience. Hayes describes six core processes of ACT: acceptance, cognitive defusion, being present, self as context, valuing, and committed action. Similarly, [researcher K.G.] Wilson et al. provides a sample model for intervention:

1. *Clients often present with a goal of erasing the past or the pain associated with it.* They have struggled for a long time with "the problem" in many different ways. Thus, avoidant behaviors are initially assessed. What has been the client's "experiential avoidance"?—that which occurs when a person is unwilling to remain in contact with particular private experiences and takes steps to alter the form or frequency of these events and the contexts that trigger them, even when doing so causes psychological harm.

2. *Examine strategies that have not worked.* The paradox is that working hard to solve the problem makes the problem seem worse. ACT sees the logic of the problem-solving system as flawed because it is based on culturally sanctioned, language-based rules for solving problems. These rules are taken for granted, such as the presence of unpleasant inner experiences (feelings, thoughts, sensations) is equivalent to a psychological problem. By default then, being healthy means the absence of these negative experiences. The ACT therapist works to challenge these rules by showing that efforts based on these rules can actually be the source of problems. A more valid and reliable source of problem solving is the client's own direct experience and their feedback from life. "It is not the client's life that is hopeless, but the strategies of experiential control (avoidance) that are hopeless."

3. *Establish control with different strategies.* A lifetime of distracting oneself from aversive private experiences is akin to constantly running away from one's shadow. The result is that in the attempt to control the negative thoughts and feelings, one is at a loss for control in other life situations.

4. *Identify that self as context, distinguished from self in content, is similar to the process of externalizing the problem in narrative approaches.* Clients are taught to get in touch with an observant self—the one that watches and experiences yet is distinct from one's inner experiences.

5. *A lack of values or a confusion of goals with values can underlie the inability to be psychologically flexible.* Thus, the next step in the ACT process is "choosing a direction and establishing willingness" and to identify motivating values and establish a willingness to help regain control of life, not necessarily just to control thoughts and feel-

ings. Willingness is not resignation, nor is it the same as wanting. It is a willingness to experience, accept, and face "negatively evaluated emotional states." Again, the difference is noted between the feeling of willingness and being willing. The example given is that you may not feel willing to go to the dentist, but you may be willing to go anyway.

6. *In the last stages of therapy, commitment is the focus.* The commitment is to give up the war of denying or fighting one's history and emotional states and find opportunities for empowering behaviors.

Techniques

With ACT, metaphors, paradoxes, and experiential exercises are frequently used. Many interventions are playful, creative, and clever. ACT protocols can vary from short interventions done in minutes to those that extend over many sessions. There are myriad techniques categorized under the following five protocols that are extrapolated from the clinical materials assembled by [researchers E.] Gifford, Hayes, and [K.] Stroshal. These represent only a fraction of material available as resources for clinicians.

1. *Facing the current situation ("creative hopelessness")* encourages clients to draw out what they have tried to make better, examine whether they have truly worked, and create space for something new to happen. Confronting the unworkable reality of their multiple experiences often leaves the client not knowing what to do next, in a state of "creative hopelessness." The state is creative because entirely new strategies can be developed without using the previous rules governing their behavior.

2. *Acceptance* techniques are geared toward reducing the motivation to avoid certain situations. An emphasis is

given to "unhooking"—realizing that thoughts and feelings don't always lead to actions. Often these techniques are done "in vivo," structuring experiences in session. Discriminating between thoughts, feelings, and experiences is a salient focus.

3. *Cognitive defusion (deliteralization)* redefines thinking and experiencing as an ongoing behavioral process, not an outcome. Techniques are designed to demonstrate that thoughts are just thoughts and not necessarily realities. It can involve sitting next to the client and putting each thought and experience out in front as an object in an effort to "defuse and deliteralize."

4. *Valuing as a choice* clarifies what the client values for his or her own sake: What gives life meaning? The goal is to help clients understand the distinction between a value and a goal, choose and declare their values, and set behavioral tasks linked to these values.

5. *Self as context* teaches the client to view his or her identity as separate from the content of his or her experience.

Potential Populations

ACT has been empirically tested, and there is reason to believe that it could be beneficial for a variety of populations. Preliminary research suggested that ACT is useful for sexual abuse survivors, at-risk adolescents, and those with substance abuse or mood disorders. Hayes suggests that the ACT model seems to be working across an unusually broad range of problems.

ACT would be appropriate for individuals with substance abuse issues, heightening motivational interviewing and enhancement approaches. ACT has been utilized with those experiencing psychotic ideation. In one study, psychiatric inpatients given ACT demonstrated improvement in affective symptoms, social impairment, and distress associated with hallucinations.

ACT has been proposed for trauma work, as well as for those with phobias and obsessive behavior. Using ACT approaches with victims of trauma seems particularly pertinent. Those who suffer from post-traumatic stress [disorder] may benefit from being able to accept the experience without resigning oneself to its residuals. The unwillingness to experience pain associated with trauma creates an internal struggle (verbal battle) that keeps the trauma alive.

For social workers dealing with survivors of childhood abuse, ACT may be a potent tool. From an ACT perspective, the cognitions and emotions that result from a history of abuse are amenable to alteration. CBT might seek to change the form of self-talk. In contrast, ACT seeks to alter the function of the thoughts and feelings. Cognitive therapy views negative thoughts and feelings in terms of their logical reasonableness; ACT focuses on their psychological reasonableness. To tell an incest survivor that her disturbing thoughts in situations of sexual intimacy are irrational is not particularly helpful. It is more useful to point out the psychological function of these thoughts.

ACT has been proposed for work with couples and families. One study demonstrated that acceptance strategies increased the effectiveness of traditional behavioral marital therapy. The goal is not to necessarily accept all partner behaviors but rather to effectively "generate a context where both accepting and changing will occur." Three ways in which ACT interventions assist couples are generating greater intimacy with the conflict area used as a vehicle, generating tolerance, and generating change. Acceptance is not accepting another's behavior, but letting go of the struggle to try to change another's behavior.

Certainly, to be proficient as an ACT therapist, training is indicated. For social workers dealing with the broad range of behavioral problems that demand short and empirically based intervention, ACT has a place. "Get off your buts" is one of the techniques used in ACT, where all "buts" are replaced with "and." So instead of saying, "I'd like to learn about ACT but don't have the time," consider saying, "I'd like to learn about ACT, and it is worth the time!"

Periodical and Internet Sources Bibliography

The following articles have been selected to supplement the diverse views presented in this chapter.

Melinda Beck	"Using Electricity, Magnets for Mental Illness," *Wall Street Journal*, January 11, 2011.
Sharon Begley	"Training Faulty Brains to Work Better," *Newsweek*, August 18, 2009.
Laura Blue	"Is Exercise the Best Drug for Depression?" *Time*, June 19, 2010.
Robert Langreth	"Patient Fix Thyself," *Forbes*, April 9, 2007.
John McManamy	"ECT—Breaking Down the Hysteria," McMan's Depression and Bipolar Web, January 12, 2011. www.mcmanweb.com.
Mark Moran	"Cognitive Therapy for Depression Effective Alternative Treatment," *Psychiatric News*, May 4, 2007.
Yvette C. Terrie	"Adherence Key to Effective Management of Schizophrenia," *Pharmacy Times*, March 1, 2008.
Shirley Wang	"Shock Value," *Washington Post*, July 24, 2007.
Chris Woolston	"Mindfulness Therapy Is No Fad, Experts Say," *Los Angeles Times*, January 8, 2011.

For Further Discussion

Chapter 1

1. Allen Frances argues that the pharmaceutical industry contributes to the spread of mental illness epidemics. Do you agree or disagree with the author? Why or why not?

2. Robert Whitaker, in his interview with Jed Lipinski, contends that psychiatric drugs are overprescribed to Americans. Mental Health America, on the other hand, alleges that some policies restrict patients' access to necessary medications. In your opinion, who makes the more compelling argument? Use examples from the texts to illustrate your position.

3. Hara Estroff Marano maintains that the connection between mental illness and creativity is commonly misunderstood. In your view, does Roger Dobson promote or undermine an understanding of genius and madness? Cite examples from the viewpoints to explain your answer.

Chapter 2

1. The Treatment Advocacy Center proposes that mental illness—not involuntary treatment—restricts civil rights. Do you agree or disagree with this view? Why or why not?

2. Norra MacReady claims that veterans with post-traumatic stress disorder may develop views that the world is a threatening place. In contrast, Paula J. Caplan states that what these individuals think and feel is normal given the horrors of war. In your opinion, who offers the more persuasive view? Provide examples from the viewpoints to support your response.

Chapter 3

1. Jeremy Olson argues that the publicity and online memorials surrounding teen suicide victims glamorize the act. Do you agree or disagree with the author? Why or why not?

2. Nathaniel S. Lehrman insists that mandatory mental health screenings at schools infringe on privacy rights. In your view, does Richard A. Friedman successfully address this concern? Why or why not?

Chapter 4

1. Melissa Dahl and Matt Snyders offer contrasting descriptions of modern-day electroconvulsive therapy sessions. In your opinion, who offers the more convincing account? Use examples from the viewpoints to explain your response.

2. Tim Calton emphasizes interpersonal relationships and respect, not medication, in the treatment of schizophrenia. In your view, does Joseph P. McEvoy uphold the role of family and dignity in his viewpoint? Why or why not?

3. Do you agree or disagree with Claudia Dewane that acceptance and commitment therapy is more effective than cognitive behavioral therapy? Why or why not?

Organizations to Contact

The editors have compiled the following list of organizations concerned with the issues debated in this book. The descriptions are derived from materials provided by the organizations. All have publications or information available for interested readers. The list was compiled on the date of publication of the present volume; the information provided here may change. Be aware that many organizations take several weeks or longer to respond to inquiries, so allow as much time as possible.

American Psychiatric Association (APA)
1000 Wilson Boulevard, Suite 1825
Arlington, VA   22209-3901
(703) 907-7300
e-mail: apa@psych.org
website: www.psych.org

An organization of psychiatrists dedicated to studying the nature, treatment, and prevention of mental disorders, the American Psychiatric Association (APA) helps create mental health policies, distributes information about psychiatry, and promotes psychiatric research and education. It publishes the *American Journal of Psychiatry* and *Psychiatric News*.

American Psychological Association (APA)
750 First Street NE, Washington, DC   20002-4242
(800) 374-2721
website: www.apa.org

With 150,000 members, the American Psychological Association (APA) is the world's largest association of psychologists. Its mission is to advance the creation, communication, and application of psychological knowledge to benefit society and improve people's lives. The association produces numerous publications, including *American Psychologist, Psychological Review*, and *Journal of Family Psychology*.

Anxiety Disorders Association of America (ADAA)
8730 Georgia Avenue, Silver Spring, MD   20910
(240) 485-1001 • fax: (240) 485-1035
website: www.adaa.org

The Anxiety Disorders Association of America (ADAA) promotes advocacy, education, training, and research for anxiety and stress-related disorders. It holds an annual conference for members and publishes position papers and the journal *Depression and Anxiety*. The ADAA website contains information on the various types of anxiety disorders.

Bazelon Center for Mental Health Law
1101 Fifteenth Street NW, Suite 1212, Washington, DC   20005
(202) 467-5730 • fax: (202)223-0409
e-mail: info@bazelon.org
website: www.bazelon.org

Bazelon Center for Mental Health Law attorneys provide technical support on mental health law issues and co-counsel selected lawsuits. The center's mission is to protect and advance the rights of adults and children who have mental disabilities, believing that they should exercise their own life choices and have access to the resources that enable them to participate fully in their communities. Its website contains news, information about specific cases, and downloadable publications.

The Carter Center
One Copenhill, 453 Freedom Parkway, Atlanta, GA   30307
(800) 550-3560
e-mail: carterweb@emory.edu
website: www.cartercenter.org

Founded by former first lady Rosalyn Carter, the Carter Center works to promote awareness, health care, and programs to support those suffering from mental illness and reduce the stigma and discrimination against them. Its Primary Care Initiative works with national experts to identify concrete action steps and deliverables to improve mental health care access and quality in the primary care setting. The center also sponsors fellowships for journalists.

Children and Adults Against Drugging America (CHAADA)
e-mail: info@chaada.org
website: www.chaada.org

Children and Adults Against Drugging America (CHAADA) is a member-based organization that aims to "raise awareness about the overmedicating of America and the deception occurring within the psychiatric profession, the inhumanity of involuntary hospitalization, the preying on innocent people, especially children, in order to turn a profit, and the dangers of the drugs used to treat alleged mental illnesses." It believes in natural healing and alternative treatments. Its website contains extensive informational material.

Law Project for Psychiatric Rights (PsychRights)
406 G Street, Suite 206, Anchorage, AK   99501
(907) 274-7686 • fax: (907) 274-9493
e-mail: query@psychrights.org
website: http://psychrights.org

The Law Project for Psychiatric Rights, also known as Psych-Rights, is a nonprofit, tax-exempt public interest law firm whose mission is to mount a strategic legal campaign against forced psychiatric drugging and electroconvulsive therapy in the United States. Its website has a vast amount of up-to-date information on legal aspects of psychiatric treatment, news, and personal stories of harm done by psychiatric drugs.

Mental Health America
2000 N. Beauregard Street, 6th Floor, Alexandria, VA   22311
(703) 684-7722 • fax: (703) 684-5968
e-mail: infoctr@mentalhealthamerica.net
website: www.mentalhealthamerica.net

Mental Health America (MHA), formerly known as the National Mental Health Association, is a nonprofit organization dedicated to helping all people live mentally healthier lives.

With more than 320 affiliates nationwide, MHA promotes the mental well-being of the nation on a daily basis and in times of crisis. MHA promotes education, research, and policy to raise awareness and assist the needs of those suffering from mental illness.

MindFreedom International (MFI)

PO Box 11284, Eugene, OR   97440-3484
(877) 623-7743 • fax: (480) 287-8833
e-mail: office@mindfreedom.org
website: www.mindfreedom.org

MindFreedom International (MFI) is an independent non-profit coalition of former psychiatric patients and their supporters that defends human rights and promotes humane alternatives for mental and emotional well-being. Its website contains information and news about the damage done by psychiatric drugs and the abuse of patients confined in psychiatric institutions.

National Institute of Mental Health (NIMH)

Science Writing, Press, and Dissemination Branch
6001 Executive Boulevard, Room 8184, MSC 9663
Bethesda, MD   20892-9663
(866) 615-6464 • fax: (301) 443-4279
e-mail: nimhinfo@nih.gov
website: www.nimh.nih.gov

The National Institute of Mental Health (NIMH) is part of the National Institutes of Health (NIH), a component of the US Department of Health and Human Services. Its mission is to transform the understanding and treatment of mental illnesses through basic and clinical research, paving the way for prevention, recovery, and cure. Its website contains news, statistics, and information about its research.

Treatment Advocacy Center

200 N. Glebe Road, Suite 730, Arlington, VA   22203
(703) 294-6001 • fax: (703) 294-6010

e-mail: info@treatmentadvocacycenter.org
website: www.treatmentadvocacycenter.org

The Treatment Advocacy Center is a national nonprofit organization dedicated to eliminating barriers to the timely and effective treatment of severe mental illnesses. It promotes laws, policies, and practices for the delivery of psychiatric care and supports the development of innovative treatments for and research into the causes of severe and persistent psychiatric illnesses. It believes that too many people with mental illness are untreated and advocates court-ordered treatment (including medication) for individuals who have a history of medication noncompliance.

Bibliography of Books

Linda Andre   *Doctors of Deception: What They Don't Want You to Know About Shock Treatment.* New Brunswick, NJ: Rutgers University Press, 2009.

Peter R. Breggin   *Your Drug May Be Your Problem:*
and David Cohen   *How and Why to Stop Taking Psychiatric Medications.* Philadelphia, PA: Da Capo Press, 2007.

Daniel Carlat   *Unhinged: The Problem with Psychiatry—A Doctor's Revelations About a Profession in Crisis.* New York: Free Press, 2010.

George   *November of the Soul: The Enigma of*
Howe Colt   *Suicide.* New York: Scribner, 2006.

Lynn E. DeLisi   *100 Questions & Answers About Schizophrenia: Painful Minds.* Sudbury, MA: Jones and Bartlett Publishers, 2011.

Duane L. Dobbert   *Understanding Personality Disorders: An Introduction.* Westport, CT: Praeger Publishers, 2010.

Kitty Dukakis   *Shock: The Healing Power of*
and Larry Tye   *Electroconvulsive Therapy.* New York: Avery, 2006.

Emily Ford with   *What You Must Think of Me: A*
Michael R.   *Firsthand Account of One Teenager's*
Liebowitz and   *Experience with Social Anxiety*
Linda Wasmer   *Disorder.* New York: Oxford
Andrews   University Press, 2007.

Richard G. Frank and Sherry A. Glied — *Better but Not Well: Mental Health Policy in the United States Since 1950.* Baltimore, MD: Johns Hopkins University Press, 2006.

Gary Greenberg — *Manufacturing Depression: The Secret History of a Modern Disease.* New York: Simon & Schuster, 2010.

Thomas Joiner — *Myths About Suicide.* Cambridge, MA: Harvard University Press, 2010.

Irving Kirsch — *The Emperor's New Drugs: Exploding the Antidepressant Myth.* New York: Basic Books, 2010.

Christopher Lukas and Henry M. Seiden — *Silent Grief: Living in the Wake of Suicide.* Philadelphia, PA: Jessica Kingsley Publishers, 2007.

Richard J. McNally — *What Is Mental Illness?* Cambridge, MA: Belknap Press of Harvard University Press, 2011.

Jonathan M. Metzel — *The Protest Psychosis: How Schizophrenia Became a Black Disease.* Boston, MA: Beacon Press, 2009.

Joshua Wolf Shenk — *Lincoln's Melancholy: How Depression Challenged a President and Fueled His Greatness.* Boston, MA: Houghton Mifflin, 2005.

Hilary Smith — *Welcome to the Jungle: Everything You Ever Wanted to Know About Bipolar but Were Too Freaked Out to Ask.* San Francisco, CA: Red Wheel/Weiser, 2010.

Kurt Snyder with Raquel E. Gur and Linda Wasmer Andrews — *Me, Myself, and Them: A Firsthand Account of One Young Person's Experience with Schizophrenia.* New York: Oxford University Press, 2007.

Jane Thompson — *Sugar & Salt: My Life with Bipolar Disorder.* Bloomington, IN: AuthorHouse, 2006.

Jean M. Twenge and W. Keith Campbell — *The Narcissism Epidemic: Living in the Age of Entitlement.* New York: Free Press, 2009.

Clint Van Winkle — *Soft Spots: A Marine's Memoir of Combat and Post-Traumatic Stress Disorder.* New York: St. Martin's Press, 2009.

Norah Vincent — *Voluntary Madness: Lost and Found in the Mental Healthcare System.* New York: Penguin, 2009.

Ethan Watters — *Crazy Like Us: The Globalization of the American Psyche.* New York: Free Press, 2010.

Robert Whitaker — *Anatomy of an Epidemic: Magic Bullets, Psychiatric Drugs, and the Astonishing Rise of Mental Illness in America.* New York: Crown Books, 2010.

Eric G. Wilson — *Against Happiness: In Praise of Melancholy.* New York: Farrar, Straus and Giroux, 2009.

Michael D. Yapko *Depression Is Contagious: How the Most Common Mood Disorder Is Spreading Around the World and How to Stop It.* New York: Free Press, 2009.

Index

W

Y

Z